JESUS
Mean
and Wild

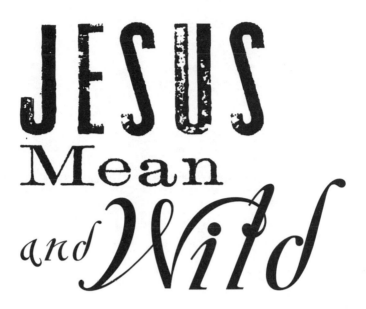

JESUS
Mean
and Wild

THE UNEXPECTED LOVE OF AN UNTAMABLE GOD

MARK GALLI

BakerBooks

Grand Rapids, Michigan

© 2006 by Mark Galli

Published by Baker Books
a division of Baker Publishing Group
P.O. Box 6287, Grand Rapids, MI 49516-6287
www.bakerbooks.com

Third printing, November 2006

Printed in the United States of America

Library of Congress Cataloging-in-Publication Data
Galli, Mark.
　　Jesus mean and wild : the unexpected love of an untamable God / Mark Galli.
　　　　p.　cm.
　　Includes bibliographical references.
　　ISBN 10: 0-8010-1284-8 (cloth)
　　ISBN 978-0-8010-1284-6 (cloth)
　　1. Jesus Christ—Character—Meditations. 2. Bible. N.T. Mark—Meditations. 3. Christian life—Meditations. I. Title.
　　BT304.G25 2006
　　232.9′03—dc22　　　　　　　　　　　　　　　　　　　2005037117

0-8010-6770-7 (intl. pbk.)
978-0-8010-6770-9 (intl. pbk.)

To Luke, Katie, and Theresa, who follow the mean and wild and merciful Jesus, each in their own delightfully unique way.

CONTENTS

FOREWORD

"I can't handle this angry, vindictive God of the Old Testament, smoke pouring out of his nostrils, coals of fire spitting from his mouth. How can you expect me to go along with such barbaric primitivism? No thanks. I'll stick with Jesus. Jesus who 'loves the little children, all the children of the world' and never raises his voice. You can have all that Old Testament yelling and stomping as far as I'm concerned. I'm a New Testament person. I'm a Jesus Christian."

How many times have you heard or even thought words like these? Maybe even said them yourself?

Not long after the Christian church was formed, men and women began talking like this. They loved Jesus but were embarrassed—scandalized is more like it—by his family. So they set about to rescue him from his heritage. They did it by the simple expedient of getting rid of it, denying that Jesus had anything to do with the God who incinerated Sodom and Gomorrah, or who established murderous, adulterous David as an ancestor of Messiah. Jesus was wonderful but he was in an entirely different class from the crude Semitic deity who created snakes and mosquitoes and terrified little children with threats of fire and brimstone.

The man who led this campaign for a nice Jesus understood Jesus as absolutely unique. He was the Savior who made all things new. In order to comprehend this uniqueness it was necessary to clear the deck of all things old. High on the list of all things old was the accumulation of crudities and barbarism that littered the pages of the Old Testament—all that anger and war, sex and superstition—so that Jesus could be seen as pure, uncompromised truth, the light-filled way of salvation, pure and simple. He vigorously waged a publicity campaign to save Jesus from every hint of divine tantrum, supernatural whim and whimsy. He wasn't content to get rid of the Old Testament; the Gospels were thoroughly contaminated by it and so had to be radically purged also. Paul was about all that was left and even he had to be edited.

It looked for a while that he might succeed. He was a powerful and influential pastor and preacher, an ardent champion of Jesus. He attracted quite a following. But then the tide turned against him. The bishop of Sinope, who was his own father, excommunicated him. The Christian community came together in a remarkable consensus and comprehensive affirmation that we cannot edit Jesus to our own convenience. We have to take the revelation as given to us by the Gospel writers, not pick and choose what pleases us, discarding the rest. The church as a whole has not wavered in that conviction.

For all his good intentions, his publicizing and promotion of Jesus as a welcome relief from the embarrassments of his family tree, Marcion (for that is the man's name) now holds the uncontested position as the church's pioneer heretic, who, in his enthusiasm for Jesus as the magnificent head of all things, tried to get rid of the earthiness of his history and the embarrassment of his family.

The ghost of Marcion is still with us.

In a free-market economy everyone is more or less free to fashion and then market whatever sells: cars, clothing, ideas, self-improvement plans, movies, books—and Jesus. When evangelism is retooled as recruitment, then marketing strategies for making Jesus attractive to a consumer spirituality begin to proliferate. Words or aspects of Jesus that carry unwelcome connotations are suppressed. We emasculate Jesus.

But we must not. Every omitted detail of Jesus, so carefully conveyed to us by the Gospel writers, reduces Jesus. We need the whole Jesus. The complete Jesus. Everything he said. Every detail of what he did.

Mark Galli, using St. Mark's Gospel as his text, is insistent that we preserve the holy angularity of Jesus who is alive among us still and wills to save us on his terms, not ours.

Eugene H. Peterson
professor emeritus of spiritual theology
Regent College, Vancouver, BC

ACKNOWLEDGMENTS

As for the communion of saints: It was Dietrich Bonhoeffer, in *Cost of Discipleship*, who showed me that grace is costly and that it is still grace. The Jesus he painted in that classic suggested to me that Jesus was more intimidating and attractive than I had imagined.

As for theological mentors: Eugene Peterson, in his writings and in conversation, has alerted me with vivid prose and incisive analysis about the dangers of sentimental discipleship—and the demands of an ever-merciful Lord.

As for friends: David Neff, editor of *Christianity Today*, gently prodded me to see the love of God in the "meanness" of Jesus, and to say what I mean and not just what sounds daring. Ted Olsen, *Christianity Today* online managing editor, has been a friendly sparring partner in many a theological debate and has sharpened my thinking as a result.

As for publishing colleagues: Bob Hosack, my editor, thankfully was not mean and wild but in fact graciously extended my writing deadline twice, and Paul Brinkerhoff gently worked with me during the editing process.

As for family: Katie has encouraged me not to mince words; she also helped me track down one nearly impossible reference. Theresa has reminded me to live with joy; she was also patient with an often distracted father (but sometimes glad of it, I suspect). Luke has reminded me that actions are as important as words; he has also given me an excuse to take much-needed breaks from writing for fly-fishing trips and golf. My wife, Barbara, has reminded me that I am loved. She was gracious enough to read the entire manuscript and "mean" enough to suggest significant rewrites here and there. The book is better for her input. But alas, the remaining flaws are my doing.

INTRODUCTION

I once wrote an article for a leading Christian publication and in one part noted how "mean" Jesus was at times. My seminary-educated editor deleted the paragraphs, and when I asked why, she said I was taking the verses out of context, and it would take too much space to explain that Jesus wasn't really mean. I replied that these were but a sampling of passages where Jesus seemed pretty intimidating. I gave two more examples. She stared at me hard. Then she blinked in seeming irritation as she said, "I can explain those too."

Every age stumbles blindly past certain teachings of Scripture. The early church didn't spend much time pondering Paul's teaching on justification by faith—that was left to the Reformation. The medieval church rarely reflected on the Great Commission—that was left to the nineteenth-century missionary movement. That movement, though strong on evangelism, was sometimes blinded by colonialism and so seemed blind to the verses about serving in love.

Today, especially in America, we have other blind spots, particularly when it comes to Jesus. Stephen Prothero, author of *American Jesus: How the Son of God Became an American Icon*, put it this way in a 1994 interview:

Christians traditionally, as they've shaped Jesus, have been worried about getting it wrong, including the Puritans. Americans today are not so worried. There isn't the sense that this is a life-and-death matter, that you don't mess with divinity. There's a freedom and even a playfulness that Americans have. . . . The flexibility our Jesus exhibits is unprecedented. There's a Gumbylike quality to Jesus in the United States. Even turning Jesus into a friend among born-again Christians—that kind of chutzpah is something that was unknown even to Americans in the Colonial period.[1]

Contra Prothero, born-again Christians are not the only ones with chutzpah. I have been a member of two mainline denominations and have heard such "Gumbylike" divinities as these: "Jesus is always patient." "Jesus's mercy embraces even the demons." "Jesus is ever-welcoming, ever-inviting, ever-affirming." Not to mention the many sermons from which I got the distinct impression that Jesus came not so much to proclaim the kingdom of heaven but to bolster my sagging self-esteem.

How foreign is all this to the Gospels? Many a *New Yorker* cartoon gently mocks the long-haired street evangelist who carries around a sign that says, "Repent! The world is about to end." But this is more or less the opening message of Jesus: "Repent, for the kingdom of heaven is at hand" (see Mark 1:15). Jesus's call to repent is stark—job, family, and former attachments must be forsaken. He never sugarcoats this call with promises of intimacy with God or having one's deepest needs met.

Nearly everywhere we turn, in the Gospel of Mark for example, we find a Jesus who storms in and out of people's lives, making implicit or explicit demands and, in general, making people feel mighty uncomfortable:

Jesus "sternly charges" or "strictly orders" (depending on the translation) people he heals (1:43; 3:12; 5:43; 8:30).

He looks upon religious leaders with "anger" and "grief" (3:5).

Jesus speaks openly of a last judgment that entails the rejection of many people (13:26–27), of a sin that God will never forgive (3:29), of horrific consequences for misleading children (9:42), of God being ashamed or severely displeased with some at the judgment (8:38; 13:36).

Jesus destroys a herd of swine, without regret or compensation to the owner (5:1–20), and overturns the tables in the temple in a moment of rage (11:15–17).

Jesus rebukes Peter as demonic (8:33). He is "indignant" with the disciples (10:13–14). He says the Sadducees are biblically and spiritually ignorant (12:24) and describes his entire generation as "faithless" (9:19).

Jesus makes it clear that following him will entail suffering and death (9:35–37, 43–50). He says the endtimes will come sooner than anyone thinks and will be so severe that even the faithful will beg for death (13:5–37).

All this, combined with Jesus's extraordinary miracles, elicits not pious peace and happiness but shock and awe. Onlookers are "amazed" at his first healing (1:27), "overcome with amazement" after the raising of the dead girl (5:42), "utterly astounded" at his walking on water (6:51), "greatly astounded" at his teaching on wealth (10:26). Even worse, the disciples are frightened after Jesus' stilling of the storm (4:35–41) and "terrified" at the transfiguration (9:6). The woman healed of a blood flow is at first filled with "fear and trembling" (5:33), and on the first Easter morning the witnesses are seized with "terror and amazement," and they run from the tomb "for they were afraid" (16:8).

This is not Jesus "meek and mild" of the infamous Wesley hymn. This is Jesus the consuming fire, the raging storm, who seems bent on destroying everything in his path, who either shocks people into stupification or frightens them so that they run for their lives. This divinity we had thought was under lock and key and confined to the Old Testament. But to find him roaming the pages of the Testament of love and forgiveness—well! And yet there he swirls, a tornado touching down, lifting homes and businesses off their foundations, leaving only bits and pieces of the former life strewn on his path.

Worse, this theme does not sit unobtrusively on the edges of biblical revelation but keeps elbowing its way onto center stage. It's not a minor aspect of God's character but a dominant personality trait. What are we to make of this? We are told—rightly!—that God is love. We are told—rightly!—that Jesus is God incarnate. How in the world are we to understand this unnerving behavior as love?

Annie Dillard writes,

> On the whole, I do not find Christians, outside of the catacombs, sufficiently sensible of conditions. Does anyone have the foggiest idea of what sort of power we so blithely invoke? Or, as I suspect, does no one believe a word of it? The churches are children playing on the floor with their chemistry sets, mixing up a batch of TNT to kill a Sunday morning. It is madness to wear ladies' straw hats and velvet hats to church; we should all be wearing crash helmets. Ushers should issue life preservers and signal flares; they should lash us to our pews.[2]

The main problem is not that we've become soft around the middle and need more stern talk of discipleship's cost or boot camps for the soul. It's not that we should resurrect the cruel and arbitrary God to inspire a proper awe of things divine. This is nothing but Christian fascism.

No, the main problem is that we've become deaf to the richer parts of the symphony of love. We hear the melody played by the strings but ignore the brass and wind and especially the percussion sections. We don't notice the strong harmonies, the counterpoint, and the dissonant chords. We are left with a memorable tune that lifts our spirits, but we are missing out on the richness of the music God would have us hear.

Catholic commentator and novelist Andrew Greeley, in a *Chicago Sun-Times* article, puts it more strongly: "Once you domesticate Jesus, he isn't there any more. The domestic Jesus may be an interesting fellow, a good friend, a loyal companion, a helpful business associate, a guarantor of the justice of your wars. But one thing he is certainly not: the Jesus of the New Testament. Once Jesus comforts your agenda, he's not Jesus anymore."[3]

For those who truly want to know and love God *as he is*, the warm and friendly Jesus, although an attractive idea, is but an idol. And the fascist God will simply not do. To enjoy a full-orbed faith will require that our idea of God gain some unnerving texture, some dynamic energy, some subtlety and depth. It will require that we live into the love of God as manifested in the mean and wild Christ. This Jesus reveals not a one-dimensional, sentimental love—a love that merely makes us feel good—but a love capable of saving a desperate world.

In this book, I explore this unnerving texture by working through seventeen passages in the Gospel of Mark where I find Jesus the most discomforting. Though I've tried to check my reading of Mark against a number of modern commentaries, this is not an exegetical book. Nor is it systematic theology. This is merely one man's attempt to understand theologically and pastorally what in the world Jesus was up to when he acted so mean and wild.

I have found time and again that as I explore this sometimes frightening mine, I spot what seems to be a speck of gold. But when I pick at it, a thick, rich vein opens up before me, and I hardly have the wherewithal to adequately excavate the brilliance that shines before me. This is not a clumsy attempt at humility but rather an encouragement to the reader ever to read, study, and inwardly digest the Gospels, where the mean and wild Jesus roams. There you will find, especially in the darkest and most forbidding passages, the very splendor and richness of God's love.

Mark Galli
St. Bartholomew's Day
AD 2005

CHAPTER 1
Difficult
Love

And a voice came from heaven, "You are my Son, the Beloved; with you I am well pleased." And the Spirit immediately drove him out into the wilderness.

Mark 1:11–12

A firefighter who can keep his cool in the kitchen is more likely to remain level-headed when things go horribly wrong at a fire.

Journalist Tom Downey[1]

God loves you and has a difficult plan for your life.

That message isn't mentioned in tracts or bestselling books. It isn't proclaimed in praise choruses or PowerPoint sermons. We've heard plenty about the god-of-the-wonderful-plan and the god-of-possibility-thinking. Recently we've been told to follow Our Bliss, which is another god disguised as the true God. And in every age, lots of people follow the god-who-will-do-well-by-me-if-I-do-well-by-him.

But the God who plans to make our lives *difficult?* And if he *really* loves us, he makes our lives *really difficult?* Yet according to the Gospels, especially Mark, this seems to be "the beginning of the good news of Jesus Christ" (Mark 1:1).

The voice ripped open the heavens to say, "You are my Son, the Beloved; with you I am well pleased" (Mark 1:11). It was as if he could hardly wait to visit a blessing on his Son. And then something heavenly settled on that tender frame. It looked like a dove—maybe like the dove that let Noah know that the drowned planet was getting a fresh start. It was like the Spirit who hovered over the original creation, as though something new, fresh, and vibrant was about to begin.

On top of that, Mark says that the words spoken to Jesus were very personal, very intimate. The Father speaks directly, perhaps affectionately, to his Son: "*You* are *my* beloved."

Beloved!

"With *you* I am well pleased."

Well pleased.

Again we hear echoes of the voice that looked over the splendor of the new creation and, on the bright dawn of the seventh day, pronounced, "It is very good" (Gen. 1:30).

Mark seems to be saying that Jesus is the Beloved, upon whom heaven is showering blessing upon blessing, before whom the future spreads out in unimaginable possibility. Is this not how the spiritual life begins for many of us?

We are baptized into the spiritual dimension. We discover God for the first time, or we accept Jesus as our personal Savior, or we are confirmed in the church. And for weeks, months, or even years, it's as if the heavens open up and the Spirit descends upon us. We relish Bible reading. Prayer is a continual joy. We gain deep insights into spiritual matters. And we actually enjoy going to church! In sermon and song and in the depths of our souls we hear and we feel that we are loved, treasured, God's own—beloved!

In the summer of 1965, my mother knelt before our black-and-white television, and following the prayer led by the image of Billy Graham flickering on the screen, she accepted Jesus into her life. My mother was not an even-keeled person. She was either up or down, and most of her life she was down: verbal abuse (and maybe worse) by parents and relatives, wild teenage years, out-of-wedlock pregnancies, one child aborted, another given up for adoption, two failed marriages, and eventually a long bout with alcoholism.

But after becoming a Christian, my mother knew *up* like she had never known up before. The joy of her salvation was unmistakable. Irritating to others sometimes, to be sure, but it was often contagious.

That's the other thing about my mother: when she was smitten with some new interest, everyone was cajoled into being smitten too. In this case, the "we" was my twelve-year-old brother, Steven, thirteen-year-old me, and my twenty-something cousin Judy, who was living with us at the time. (My even-keeled father was the exception; he'd gotten used to Mom's enthusiasms and had learned to ignore most of them.) Over the next few months, she dragged us to the local Evangelical Free Church for Sunday morning worship. And Sunday evening worship. And Wednesday evening prayer meetings—unless we happened to be at church already for a week-long missions conference or revival.

On our spare nights, Mom gathered us around the dinner table for Bible study and prayer. For at least an hour or two. Every night. For four months. Enveloped by both my mother's cigarette smoke and the Holy Spirit, we argued about passages from the Gospel of John, wondered aloud about spiritual matters, and prayed—and then basked in many answers to prayer.

One of the astounding miracles of those months was this: to this day I do not recall ever feeling resentful, put upon, or rebellious—and I was thirteen at the time! What's with that?

Well, it was our baptism into things spiritual, and like Jesus coming out of the water, it was as if heaven was ripped open for the sole purpose of showering blessing upon blessing on us. God seemed to have nothing but a wonderful plan for us. We knew, without a doubt, that we were beloved.

Most Bible versions put a visual break—an extra space or new heading—after Jesus's baptism. As a result, we don't usually connect the baptism with what comes next. But there is no break in the ancient manuscripts. Immediately after the glorious baptism comes this: "And the Spirit immediately drove him out into the wilderness" (Mark 1:12).

This is the same Spirit who just a moment earlier was the visible image of the Father's love, sent by the Father to show Jesus he is beloved, pleasing, a splendor to behold, symbolizing the pristine beginning of something wonderfully new. Now this Spirit drives the beloved Son into the desert. Literally, in the Greek in which this was written, Jesus is "cast out" from the warmth of home and friends, from the comforts of town and village. He is denied even moral and spiritual support—the Torah, the synagogue, the wisdom of the town elders, even, it seems, the comfort of the heavenly Father's presence. Jesus is driven into the wilderness, deserted by love, to face a hostile adversary alone.

And not just any adversary, but the most powerful and sinister of enemies. Mark's version of Jesus's temptation doesn't tell us much about the strategy of this Evil One as do Matthew and Luke. For Mark it is enough to describe his fearsome incarnation: if the Spirit comes to Jesus in the form of a dove, satanic temptation comes to him in the form of wild beasts.

This temptation was severe—forty days and forty nights of fasting, a thorough and complete period of rigorous self-denial. On top of that, there were those beasts. But what exactly were they? They could have been physical—boars, snakes, or whatever. But it could be that the beasts were not merely outside of Jesus's body but also inside Jesus's head, like the experience of Antony of the Desert.

Antony was a young Egyptian Christian who, upon hearing the Scripture about forsaking wealth and family to follow Christ, did just that. Sometime around AD 285 he sold his possessions, put his sister into the care of friends, and walked out into the desert to pray and meditate to learn the spiritual life.

Athanasius, Antony's biographer, describes not only his triumphs but also his most severe temptations. In one series of hallucinations, it seems that Antony's sanity is on the line:

> The demons . . . were changed into forms of beasts and reptiles. The place was immediately filled with the appearance of lions, bears, leopards, bulls, and serpents, asps, scorpions, and wolves, and each of these moved in accordance with its form. The lion roared, wanting to spring at him; the bull seemed intent on goring; the creeping snake did not quite reach him; the onrushing wolf made straight for him—and altogether the sounds of all the creatures that appeared were terrible, and their ragings were fierce.[2]

Don't many of our temptations take such forms? Do we sometimes hear the roar of condemnation for past sins, feel gored by remorse, and sense hope itself slip away because of the terrible and fierce ragings within? Indeed, if Jesus was tempted in every way like us, he was surely tempted by wild beasts just as fierce.

Mark seems to be saying something startling in his stark account: God so loved his Son that he sent him into a kind of hell.

God did this to Jesus, his *beloved*?

The mind reels. A love that casts out? A love that withdraws all loving presence? A love that drives us to the limits of sanity?

During World War II, a Russian brigadier commander called a captain to his headquarters and immediately asked him for his pistol. The captain suspected nothing and handed it over to him. Immediately from a corner of the room, two counterintelligence officers bounded across the floor and grabbed the captain, tearing at the star in his cap, his shoulder boards, his officer's belt.

"You are under arrest!" they shouted.

"Me? For what?"

Indeed, for what? He was the son of a patriot, a man who had served his nation in World War I. He himself had served with distinction for four years, having just ten days earlier led his reconnaissance battery nearly intact under heavy fire.

In his youth all he had wanted to be was a writer. The early death of his father required him to be of more practical help to his mother, and he earned a mathematics degree. He had been teaching physics in a high school and taking a correspondence course in writing when he was called up for service in 1941. The war was now drawing to a close, and he looked forward to returning to his teaching, to his writing, and to his wife. For what, then, had he been arrested?

Usually, the reasons for arrest remained unspoken, but as the captain was being led away, the commander ordered him to come back and hinted at the charge: "You have a friend on the First Ukrainian Front?"

The captain immediately knew the problem. He had written a school friend, criticizing Joseph Stalin. Given the oppressive climate of 1940s Russia, his hopes for a normal life vanished. He was to face eight years in prison and then decades of exile from his homeland.

The habitually severe commander, realizing what lay before the captain, mustered up a measure of pity, saying, "I wish you happiness, Captain."[3]

For most of us most of the time, life is glorious and good. It is punctuated with births and baptisms, with graduations and weddings, with falling in love and sexual ecstasy. We know our fair share of acing finals and getting promotions. We relish deep roast coffee in the morning and a rib roast dinner at night, sweet success in the marketplace and sweet fellowship in the home. And this is not to mention spiritual blessings that shower upon us after conversion, a life-changing retreat, or a special season of prayer.

But then come the interruptions to joy. It doesn't necessarily happen suddenly, shockingly, as it did for future Nobel Prize–winning author Aleksandr Solzhenitsyn, the captain described above. For me it was not nearly so terrifying but nonetheless painful.

The years following my family's blissful conversion—well, let's just say it was sometimes hard to discern God's wonderful plan. We wandered aimlessly from church to church because, said my mother, each one was full of hypocrites. Steven drifted into drug abuse. My parents divorced, then got together, then had affairs, and then, just when they were beginning to get it together, my mother had a heart attack and died at age fifty-seven. In the meantime, I battled doubts about God's existence and the value of my marriage and endured a low-grade depression for years.

I won't bore you with more details. To be sure, I knew nothing as horrific as brutal imprisonment. I note both Solzhenitsyn's experience and mine because they represent the poles of difficulty that life hands us. Mine ordinary, his extraordinary, both miserable in their own way.

What this passage teaches is that this pattern is not an accident. Sometimes God drives us into trials and tribulations, as he did with Jesus. Sometimes he merely allows evil days to overshadow us. In either case, we move from spiritual bliss to moments of misery by God's providence.

We are desperate to spare God from any blame: "What kind of God would let such things happen on his watch?" Well, certainly not the god-of-the-twenty-first-century. He is a kind, benevolent being who knows nothing of discipline, character, or tough love. He's a softy who sheds tears at our suffering and tries to give us brief moments of comfort and courage but in the end is powerless to do anything else.

This, in my view, is a pretty worthless god, a passive, impotent deity who helplessly watches his creation fall apart before his eyes. Unfortunately, this god is often presented as the deity of the Christian faith, the God and Father of our Lord Jesus Christ. Fortunately, a reading of the Bible shows this to be a lie. This passage in the Gospel of Mark (1:9–13) is but one example that God is anything but impotent, anything but passive, and anything but a softy.

He is instead a God who is in control of history and is in control of our lives. Indeed, he is gentle and merciful and kind. But he is also strong to save. And he loves us so much he refuses to pamper us.

Aleksandr Solzhenitsyn went on to become arguably one of the most influential writers of the twentieth century, the author of the massive *The Gulag Archipelago*, which brought to the world's attention the ravages of Soviet communism. In volume 2, he describes a moving encounter with a Christian inmate and his subsequent murder, and how that startled Solzhenitsyn out of his self-pity. In a poem, he depicts his life before prison as one of pride and self-assurance, and then he notes how close he came to death, both physical and spiritual. He admits that it wasn't because of "good judgment" or "desire" that he became aware but only by "the even glow of the Higher Meaning." He concludes,

> And now with measuring cup returned to me,
> Scooping up living water,
> God of the Universe! I believe again!
> Though I renounced You, You were with me![4]

Solzhenitsyn believes that the most significant consequence of his suffering is a renewed relationship with God. But he also mentions something more that God's angels did for him:

> It would seem that in this situation, feelings of malice, the disturbance of being oppressed, aimless hate, irritability, and nervousness ought to multiply. But you yourself do not notice how, with the impalpable flow of time, slavery nurtures in you the shoots of contradictory feelings. . . .
>
> Formerly you never forgave anyone. You judged people without mercy. And you praised people with equal lack of moderation. And now an understanding mildness has become the basis of your uncategorical judgments. You have come to realize your own weaknesses—and you can therefore understand the weaknesses of others. . . .
>
> Your soul, which formerly was dry, now ripens from suffering.[5]

Suffering indeed grants us a renewed spiritual vitality and strengthened character—this is a commonplace, though one that has to be learned again and again. The one problem is that this view of suffering, if left to itself, makes suffering ultimately about us. But there is a more excellent way.

In a *New York Times* opinion piece, Tom Downey defends the hazing that firemen endure when they enter the ranks of that noble profession. Downey is a documentary filmmaker and a writer who studied New York firefighters to prepare for a project. New recruits earn the respect of veterans, he says, "by enduring the silent treatment, tolerating jeers about their masculinity and bravery," and performing menial tasks like taking out the garbage and cleaning toilets.[6]

Like soldiers, he explains, firefighters see things that nobody else wants to: burnt bodies, anguished people who have lost their dearest possessions, best friends dead at an early age. Then these firemen have to somehow put these experiences on a mental shelf and go home and be good husbands and fathers. "Make no mistake," Downey says, "this is a job that exacts a tremendous psychological toll."

Add to that the physical toll of smoke headaches, sore joints, cuts and bruises from smashing in doors and windows, lungs filled with black mucus, and a nausea that can make a man bend over and vomit. Downey describes one veteran who saved a baby by dragging a crib out of a room so hot that the crib melted in his hands and another who badly scorched his lungs when he ran into a burning room without an air tank to save a young man.

Communities need men like these, men willing to risk life or serious injury in order save others. "Amid all the hazing," Downey writes, "firefighters are really seeking an answer to a simple question: Is this the guy I want coming down the hallway for me if I get trapped in a burning building?"

The banter that flies across the kitchen table at firehouses can be crude, and no doubt hazing in general can step over the line. But, Downey argues, the taunts strengthen and prepare the men for working in danger. "A firefighter who can keep his cool in the kitchen," he says, "is more likely to remain level-headed when things go horribly wrong at a fire."

It is not an accident that right after Mark notes that the angels minister to Jesus (Mark 1:13), he goes forth into Galilee preaching, teaching, and healing. In other words, by God's design, Jesus's misery prepared him for his ministry. The writer of Hebrews puts it this way: "Because he himself was tested by what he suffered, he is able to help those who are being tested" (Heb. 2:18). Paul talks about this in his second letter to the Corinthian church: "Blessed be the God and Father of our Lord Jesus Christ, the Father of mercies and the God of all consolation, who consoles us in all our affliction, so that we may be able to console those who are in any affliction" (2 Cor. 1:3–4). This is one reason Solzhenitsyn was able to go on to write and speak from the heart of the Gulag and embolden millions to fight tyranny despite insufferable conditions and insurmountable odds.

Suffering is our preparation for ministry in a world of suffering—all manner of suffering: from the trivial irritations of daily life to paralyzing accidents, from family squabbles to church splits, from the ravages of sexual slavery to the countless deaths of innocents at the hands of cruel dictators. This is not a world for shallow people with soft character. It needs tested, toughened disciples who are prepared, like their Lord, to descend into hell to redeem the lost.

To be sure, some suffering remains an unfathomable mystery of pain. Still, many of the difficulties that God sometimes directs and sometimes permits in our lives make some sense when seen in this redemptive light. And such suffering is about more than character. God's got the whole world in his mind, and he is looking for people who are keeping that world foremost in their minds as well.

Often when I present this line of thought to friends, when I emphasize what suffering does for us and others, someone will invariably joke, "Ah yes, but who really wants to grow in character and love?" We all chuckle, but we are only relieving the tension of having just recognized again the selfishness that grips us.

Certainly some suffering cannot be avoided, but when I have a choice in the matter, I invariably take the easy way out. Take something trivial. Gluttony is a sin by which I'm regularly tempted—not mere overeating, but overeating as a way to numb stress and anxiety. It's a common habit in our culture precisely because it works, at least in the short run. When I'm anxious about some matter, I seek out food and drink, among other pleasurable activities, to distract me from my pain.

A wiser and harder course is to think and pray about the pain, seeking to understand myself better and putting my life again into the hands of God's loving care. But that requires my spending time in the pain to experience it, to endure it. And that I'm usually not willing to do. So I run from it, even though living through it will help me grow up in Christ and eventually can be used in some way to help others.

If I'm unable to live faithfully in this minor suffering, what am I going to do when something bigger overwhelms me? I'll probably do what most of us do: I'll whine and complain about the injustice of life or the cruelty of God. This despite the consistent witness of Scripture that God's plan for us is a difficult one and that redemption—personal, social, and spiritual—does not happen without suffering.

Paul had the deeper perspective: "I want to know Christ and the power of his resurrection and the sharing of his sufferings by becoming like him in his death" (Phil. 3:10). I love that first part: to know the power of Christ's resurrection. But how casually I ignore the truth that I can never know Christ's life and power unless I come also to know his sufferings and death.

This is but one of the ways the untamable love of God surprises us. Difficulties and sufferings are God's form of hazing. Sometimes it gets so bad, we think he is cruel. But he's only working to fashion men and women who will keep their cool when things go horribly wrong, people prepared to dash into burning rooms to rescue those about to be engulfed in flames.

CHAPTER 2
A Hopeful Repentance

Now after John was arrested, Jesus came to Galilee, proclaiming the good news of God, and saying, "The time is fulfilled, and the kingdom of God has come near; repent, and believe in the good news."

Mark 1:14–15

It is a spiritual gift from God for a man to perceive his sins.

St. Isaac of Syria[1]

The Book of Common Prayer (1928) includes a general confession that was to be prayed daily by faithful Episcopalians:

Almighty and most merciful Father; We have erred, and strayed from thy ways like lost sheep. We have followed too much the devices and desires of our own hearts. We have offended against thy holy laws. We have left undone those things we ought to have done; And we have done those things which we ought not to have done; And there is no health in us. But thou, O Lord, have mercy upon us, miserable offenders.[2]

This is just the sort of negativity—"no health in us," "miserable offenders"—that we today associate with the word *repentance*, and it's one reason we've worked mightily to banish that word from the English vocabulary.

I look at my life some days and it's hard to imagine that I am a *miserable* offender and that there is *no health* in me. I go to church. I read my Bible. I help at the homeless shelter once a month. At home, I do the dishes, take out the trash, and don't beat my children. I don't even ground them. Most nights, when I close my day with prayer (see there, regular prayer—another jewel in my crown), I usually have nothing but peccadilloes to confess—a little sloth here, some impatience there.

For others the problem with repentance runs deeper. They have been raised in legalistic environments and carry around a guilt-laden backpack that would bend the knees of a Himalayan Sherpa. And most of the guilt, they realize, is neurotic—not based on any real transgression, but the product of defective discipleship. Years of "Christian nurture" has contorted their souls. So after drinking a glass of wine or failing to say the rosary or breaking one of a thousand other man-made religious taboos, they cannot shake the pangs of miserable guilt. If this is what repentance conjures up, they are right to want nothing of it.

Others still fight not false guilt but spiritual despair. They believe, rightly so, that true religion is about love and grace. But they've heard a rumor that the Lord is a holy God, and they suspect that they just may be miserable sinners. So they spend their days making sure these two combustible ideas never mix—something repentance tries to do—because if they ever did, such people fear that the resulting explosion would blow their faith to smithereens.

Add to this the twentieth-century fascination with self-esteem and a society hooked on affirmation steroids, and it is no wonder that we have created a faith that can hardly pronounce the word.

To the modern reader, then, Jesus's opening words seem odd at best. The substance of his message he calls "good news" (Mark 1:15). These two words refer back to the first part of the sentence, which says that it is a glorious time, a time when things will be set right with the planet. The "kingdom of God" and "good news" act like bookends.

Yet what lies between the bookends doesn't seem like good news: "repent and believe." *Believe*—okay, we can try to muster that up. We know that distracted, doubting, but basically together people like us need the occasional pep talk, "You gotta believe," "Have faith," "Trust!"

On the other hand, *repent* is not a word one uses in polite company anymore. Comedians bark it to mock the self-righteous. Cartoonists picture a disheveled, bearded man carrying a sign that says, "Repent! The world is about to end"—add a clever caption and you have a guaranteed laugh. But it just wouldn't do for a preacher in most churches today to use the word in a serious vein.

It's apparent, however, that Jesus is not playing the comic here. And he is anything but a self-righteous hypocrite. *Repent* is a word that not only begins Jesus's ministry, it is one of the last things he has to say when, in the book of Revelation, he addresses wayward churches, saying, "Remember then from what you have fallen; *repent*" (Rev. 2:5).

The early church picked up Jesus's cue and made repentance a central feature of its faith. It is one of the most common words in the New Testament, occurring in one form or another over fifty times. Peter concludes the first Christian sermon not by painting a picture of God's unconditional love but by exhorting his listeners, "Repent, and be baptized every one of you in the name of Jesus Christ so that your sins may be forgiven; and you will receive the gift of the Holy Spirit" (Acts 2:38).

Later Peter urges another crowd, "Repent therefore, and turn to God so that your sins may be wiped out" (Acts 3:19), and later explains in his epistle, "The Lord is not slow about his promise, as some think of slowness, but is patient with you, not wanting any to perish, but all to come to repentance" (2 Peter 3:9). And lest anyone be confused about what he means by *perish*, he adds, "But the day of the Lord will come like a thief, and then the heavens will pass away with a loud noise, and the elements will be dissolved with fire, and the earth and everything that is done on it will be disclosed" (2 Peter 3:10).

Paul speaks with similar gravity. "While God has overlooked the times of human ignorance," he tells the pagan Athenians, "now he commands all people everywhere to repent, because he has fixed a day on which he will have the world judged in righteousness by a man whom he has appointed" (Acts 17:30–31).

It is also a common theme for Paul. The "apostle of grace" is more than happy to describe the essence of his ministry by saying that he "declared first to those in Damascus, then in Jerusalem and throughout the countryside of Judea, and also to the Gentiles, that they should repent and turn to God and do deeds consistent with repentance" (Acts 26:20). In fact the early church as a whole didn't have a problem summarizing the Christian message in just this way, calling it "the repentance that leads to life" (Acts 11:18).

The *way* that leads to life—that's what we'd expect to hear. The *spirituality* that leads to life—we like that. But the *repentance* that leads to life?

When Jesus connects *kingdom of God* with *good news* with *repentance*, he is doing the same thing. Jesus seems mean and wild, off-putting and preposterous, disagreeable to modern sensibilities.

The story is told that when the desert father Abba Sisoes was about to die, he had visions of prophets and saints visiting him. The desert fathers who were with him asked, "Show us with whom you are speaking, father."

Abba Sisoes said, "Behold, the angels came to take me away, and I asked them to leave me so that I might tarry here a little longer and repent."

The fathers were startled because they thought that Abba Sisoes had long since achieved holiness. He had been a desert monk—praying, fasting, and praying some more—for seventy-two years. They said to him, "You have no need to repent, father."

Abba Sisoes replied, "I do not know in my soul if I have rightly begun to repent." At this, the story goes, they all realized that the old man was perfect.[3]

This old story of the saint illustrates a long-standing fact, one that applies even in the postmodern age: there is never a day we don't need to repent.

I wish I could foist this repentance business off to the beginning of the Christian walk, as if pagans are the only people who need to repent. I wish I could say that after becoming a Christian as a teenager, I suddenly began thinking clearly and living righteously. But in our most honest moments, we know that Paul took the words right out of our mouths: "I do not do the good I want, but the evil I do not want is what I do. . . . I delight in the law of God in my inmost self, but I see in my members another law at war with the law of my mind. . . . Wretched man that I am!" (Rom. 7:19, 22–24).

The fact that some days I can hardly imagine my need to repent just shows how shallow my faith has become—as if it's mostly about religious and social graces and the occasional act of mercy. And though we are right to eschew false guilt and debilitating shame, there remains plenty of true guilt and healthy shame that we need to deal with all our lives.

One thing that can help us restore the word *repentance* to our vocabulary is to remember what it means. Contrary to the popular imagination, the word *repent* stands for a very healthy idea. To repent means to change one's mind, to turn around and go in a different direction, to start thinking and living differently.

"The first step toward God is a step away from the lies of the world," says Eugene Peterson in his classic *A Long Obedience in the Same Direction*. "It is a renunciation of the lies we have been told about ourselves and our neighbors and our universe." And the typical biblical word to describe this process is *repentance*. "It is always and everywhere the first word in the Christian life."[4]

Repentance is not so much an emotion or feeling sorry, though it does include that. Instead, as Peterson puts it, "it is deciding that you have been told a pack of lies about yourself and your neighbor and your world. And it is deciding that God in Jesus Christ is telling you the truth. Repentance is a realization that what God wants from you and what you want from God are not going to be achieved by doing the same old things, thinking the same old thoughts."

And so one of the first lies we must renounce is that repentance is outdated or irrelevant.

"Shame indeed there is when each makes known his sins," writes the early church father, Ambrose, "but that shame, as it were, ploughs his land, removes the ever-recurring brambles, prunes the thorns, and gives life to the fruits which he believed were dead.... If you plough after this fashion you will sow spiritual seed. Plough that you may get rid of sin and gain fruit."[5]

Though repentance is mostly a decision, it nonetheless involves uncomfortable emotions. This is one reason we avoid it. But if we run from this pain, we run from redemption.

Without wallowing in guilt and shame, we can and must explore the pain because those discomforting feelings point us to areas where the Spirit of Jesus is working on us. We have courage to explore the pain because we know that Jesus's harsh word of repentance is set on a foundation of grace.

When Jesus calls us to repent, he's announcing that we are thinking and behaving badly. We are going in a wrong and destructive direction. When we look deeply and honestly at our lives, we admit, as have all deeply spiritual people in history, that we really are miserable sinners who have "no health" in us. This does not mean that there is no good within us, for we simply don't have the power to wipe away every shred of goodness that God has created in us. The fact that we know we're spiritually unhealthy, for instance, is a sign of some spiritual health. What that phrase means is this: We are so spiritually sick, we can do nothing to make ourselves well. Our case is terminal—without outside aid we will perish.

So, like Paul, we sometimes cry out that we are wretched and wonder "Who will rescue me from this body of death?" (Rom. 7:24). But once we remember the gospel, we will also cry out with Paul, "Thanks be to God through Jesus Christ our Lord!" (Rom. 7:25). This is not simply because Jesus died on the cross for our sins and daily offers us the opportunity to repent. The contemporary Orthodox writer Frederica Mathewes-Green puts it this way:

> Jesus didn't come to save us just from the *penalty* for our sins; he came to save us from our *sins*—now, today, if we will only respond to the challenge and let him. . . . The Lord does not love us for our good parts and pass over the rest. He died for the bad parts and will not rest until they are put right. We must stop thinking of God as infinitely indulgent. We must begin to grapple with the scary and exhilarating truth that he is infinitely holy, and that he wants the same for us.[6]

To put it another way, it's as if we've made the team. During tryouts, we are judged severely. Coaches look at our every move. After we've made the team, our every move is still critiqued, but the ground has shifted. It is no longer a matter of making the team but of excelling. It is certainly painful to be reminded of a mistake (like missing a tackle that leads to an opponent's touchdown) or to endure a coach's dressing down. But when such things happen, wise athletes don't go into a funk, wallowing in their mistakes. They let the shame and guilt do its work: motivate them to play better.

"Not that I have already . . . reached the goal," says Paul in his own sports analogy, "but I press on to make it my own, because Christ Jesus has made me his own. Beloved, I do not consider that I have made it my own; but this one thing I do: forgetting what lies behind and straining forward to what lies ahead, I press on toward the goal for the prize of the heavenly call of God in Christ Jesus" (Phil. 3:12–14).

"Some one will say: 'We have been beguiled and are lost. Is there then no salvation left? We have fallen: Is it not possible to rise again? We have been blinded: May we not recover our sight? We have become crippled: Can we never walk upright? In a word, we are dead: May we not rise again?'"[7]

This very modern sentiment—this despair at failing Christ so often—is expressed by Cyril, archbishop of Jerusalem (AD 315–386). After recognizing the despair with which repentance often tempts us, he says, "Will not He that raised Lazarus, already four days dead and fetid, far more easily raise you? He who poured out His precious blood for us will free us from sin. Let us not despair, brethren; nor give ourselves up as lost. For it is a grievous thing not to believe in the hope of repentance."

CHAPTER 3
Holy War

Just then there was in their synagogue a man with an unclean spirit, and he cried out, "What have you to do with us, Jesus of Nazareth? Have you come to destroy us? I know who you are, the Holy One of God." But Jesus rebuked him, saying, "Be silent, and come out of him!" And the unclean spirit, convulsing him and crying with a loud voice, came out of him.

Mark 1:23–26

It is by warfare that the soul makes progress.

Abba John the Dwarf[1]

"We are only 500 yards from the beach and are ordered to get down. Minutes later the boat stops and begins to toss in the waves. The ramp goes down and without hesitation my section leader, Corporal John Gibson, jumps out well over his waist in water. He only makes a few yards and is killed. We have landed dead on into a pillbox with a machine gun blazing away at us."[2]

This is the recollection of Jim Wilkins, of the Queen's Own Rifles of Canada, B Company, on June 6, 1944—D-day. As soon as Wilkins splashes into the water, "something hit my left magazine pouch and stops me up short for a moment. The round had gone right through two magazines, entered my left side and came out my back."

"Come on! Come on!" yells his gun mate, Kenny.

"I'm coming! I'm coming!" Wilkins yells back.

They are now up to their knees in water. He recalls, "You can hear a kind of buzzing sound all around, as well as the sound of the machine gun itself. All of a sudden something slapped the side of my right leg and then a round caught me dead centre up high on my right leg causing a compound fracture. By this time, I was flat on my face in the water—I've lost my rifle, my helmet is gone and Kenny is still yelling at me to come on."

The synagogue service in Capernaum (Mark 1:23–26) is Jesus's D-day, his beach landing to recapture lost territory, a battle with the forces of evil that rain down terror on him, the beginning of eschatological war, the "clearing the earth of demons."[3]

We see a more detailed and dramatic account of Jesus's hand-to-hand combat with demons in Mark 5:1–20. There the possessed man is one who spends "night and day among the tombs . . . always howling and bruising himself with stones" (v. 5). He is a man who, like the man in the Capernaum synagogue, is both attracted to and frightened by Jesus. He rushes up to Jesus and screams for his life, "What have you to do with me, Jesus, Son of the Most High God? I adjure you by God, do not torment me!" (v. 7).

In both scenes Jesus reigns victorious—a foreshadowing of his ultimate victory over evil on the cross and at the end of history. But one cannot help but recognize that the plight of the demoniac is an especially dramatic metaphor of anyone in whom the battle of good and evil rages and in whom evil seems to be winning, when we feel we are up to our knees in water, a great buzzing sound all around, crawling up a beach with a shattered leg while a machine gun continually tries to take us out—death, fatigue, and confusion all around. Is this not at times a nearly perfect description of the spiritual life?

This, once again, is not the way the spiritual life is usually marketed. Mostly we hear about the wonderful life, the best life, the blessed life. We are assaulted with messages about grace and love, sweetness and light, freedom and peace—all of which pass understanding. And all of this is true in some respects, thank God. But we risk lying to others, we risk lying to ourselves, if we don't fill out this picture.

Normandy today is a beautiful stretch of beach and countryside, white sand, blue water, rolling hills of green as you look up from the shore. Today it the very picture of peace and freedom. In June 1944 it was anything but that. Then it was a contested land in the hands of a totalitarian regime. It became what it is today only as the result of, as Winston Churchill put it, blood, toil, tears, and sweat.

Mark's view is that the Christian life is in large part a battle. John begins his Gospel with a wedding feast, reminding us of the joy of the kingdom. Matthew begins with the Sermon on the Mount, pointing to the kingdom's radical ethic. Luke begins with the synagogue sermon, highlighting that the kingdom is for rich and poor, Jew and Gentile. Mark begins with a confrontation with a demoniac to show how kingdom life begins—with a violent assault on evil by the Holy One.

This is not an accident. The angel announces that the child Mary carries will be called holy (Luke 1:35). Peter calls Jesus the "Holy One" (John 6:68–69). And the early church says he "was declared to be Son of God with power according to the spirit of holiness by resurrection from the dead" (Rom. 1:4) and that "Christ Jesus . . . became for us wisdom from God, and righteousness and sanctification" (1 Cor. 1:30).

Jesus's mission then and now very simply is this: to make the unclean holy. In this he merely incarnates the work of

God begun centuries earlier with the Hebrews: "You shall be holy, for I the LORD your God am holy" (Lev. 19:2). Thus the demoniac has it exactly right when he calls Jesus "the Holy One of God" (Mark 1:24) and assumes that he is out to destroy evil.

We tend to think of the pursuit of holiness as the legalistic hobby of people like the Pharisees. So we often hear the grace of Jesus pitted against the Pharisees' concern for ritual cleanness. However, Jesus never criticizes the Pharisees for the nature of their concerns, only the depth of them. He expects his disciples to be holy: "For I tell you, unless your righteousness exceeds that of the scribes and Pharisees, you will never enter the kingdom of heaven" (Matt. 5:20).

The difference between Jesus's holiness ethic and that of the Pharisees is this: the Pharisees refuse to touch any unclean thing. Jesus aims to make the unclean holy.

Paul, the "apostle of grace" as he is often called, understood this as central to his ministry as well. More popular readings of Paul's letter to the Romans take it to be about grace. Indeed, but grace that is moving forward: "But thanks be to God that you, having once been slaves of sin, have become obedient from the heart to the form of teaching to which you were entrusted, and that you, having been set free from sin, have become slaves of righteousness" (Rom. 6:17–18).

To be holy means to be set apart for divine purposes. God wants nothing less than all creation, which is now subject to decay, futility, and corruption, to become sanctified, alive, and completely dedicated to his purposes. This aspect of holiness has two dimensions: the shaping of our character to be set apart in godliness and the shaping of our calling so that our lives will be set apart for God's purposes. In short, to be holy is to dedicate all that we are and all that we do to God.

✠

I had a friend some years ago who would simply not let Jesus in, at least not all the way. He was a good Christian by all outward appearances. He was a faithful elder in his church and a devoted husband and father. He had a reputation for honesty, courage, and integrity. But he once confided in me that he was conflicted about his use of pornography.

He said he wasn't addicted, and there was no reason not to believe him. He could go weeks without indulging, he said. It didn't affect his relationship with his wife. It didn't interfere with his church work or prayer life. It was to him a little recreational pleasure that he indulged in now and then, especially when he wanted to reward himself after working long and hard for his company or his church.

"I've justified it in my mind a thousand times," he explained, "and I could out-argue anyone who wants to give me all that bull about potential addiction and/or it ruining your marriage. Well, to be frank, it's only made my marriage easier, since I don't pester my wife as often, and yet I don't do porn so much that I don't have any ardor for her when she's ready to do it."

"Still," he concluded, "I feel so unclean."

That didn't make sense to him, since he had so persuasively rationalized his behavior. At first he thought it was just left-over guilt from his fundamentalist upbringing. But he noticed he didn't feel residual guilt about other postfundamentalist behavior, such as drinking wine or going to the movies. Still, pornography continued to make him feel "unclean."

I suggested that this feeling might be the prodding of the Spirit. "Why don't you just give it up?"

"I've thought about that," he replied. "But here's the most irrational thing. If God does want me to give it up, I know he wants it because it's ultimately good for me. Yet the thought of giving up porn cold turkey, just stop and no more—that's one of the most frightening things I can imagine right now. And I don't know why."

My friend was experiencing an age-old and very common human struggle—this irrational sense that our sins are so much a part of us we can't imagine living without them. Augustine eloquently described this tension in his *Confessions*: "For out of the perverse will came lust, and the service of lust ended in habit, and habit, not resisted, became necessity." And when he started to ponder giving up these "necessities," he said, "Unruly habit kept saying to me, 'Do you think you can live without them?'"[4]

This is one reason a life of holiness frightens us, why an encounter with the real Jesus can be so unnerving. When he comes into our presence, we sense the chasm between his holiness and our uncleanness. There is a palpable sense that unholiness cannot be in God's holy presence and live (Exod. 33:20). Isaiah trembles at his encounter with God: "Woe is me! I am lost, for I am a man of unclean lips" (Isa. 6:5). And the man in the synagogue, when meeting the Holy One of God, shouts, "Have you come to destroy us?" (Mark 1:24).

Again, the way we've marketed the faith, this doesn't make sense. Isn't Jesus the warm and welcoming presence who accepts all and forgives all and into whose arms we confidently go? Indeed, this is precisely why the man in the synagogue and the man who lived among the tombs (Mark 5:1–17) both rush to be in Jesus's presence. Jesus is immensely attractive to us, someone who calls something deep within us to himself, someone from whom we have nothing to hide, someone who simply loves us.

But we misconstrue his love—we may even be attracted to a mere figment of our imagination—if we don't also sense fear. The one who loves us is the Holy One who wishes to make all unclean things holy. That means the one whom we cannot stay away from is the same one who is out to destroy those very habits, sins, notions, addictions, and self-justifications that we think we can't live without. And there are times when we feel as if Jesus is out to destroy us.

It is a wonderful *and* a fearful thing to fall into the hands of the real Jesus.

Jesus "torments" us not merely to set apart our character but also our calling. This too can be a fearful thing.

Hudson Taylor had first set foot in China as a twenty-one-year-old neophyte missionary in 1854. But his early evangelistic passion was exhausted in seven years, and he returned to England to recover. His brief bout with burnout did not extinguish the evangelistic flame within. The more he reflected on the spiritual situation in China, the more the flame was fanned and the deeper his anxiety grew. Toward the end of his sabbatical, Taylor wrote a book that explored the issues he wrestled with his entire time in England. In *China: Its Spiritual Needs and Claims*, he alternately chastised and pleaded with the West:

> Can all the Christians of England sit still with folded arms while these multitudes are perishing—perishing for lack of knowledge—for lack of that knowledge which England possesses so richly, which had made England what England is and made us what we are? What does the Master teach us? Is it not that if one sheep out of a hundred be lost, we are to leave the ninety and nine and seek that one? But here the proportions are almost reversed, and we stay at home with the one sheep, and take no heed to the ninety and nine perishing ones![5]

Yet Taylor cowered at the idea of starting a missions agency that would, contrary to the current practice in China, place people in the vast interior where most Chinese lived. To subject young men and women to a life of debilitating illness and social rejection, even persecution—the very things he endured in his seven-year stint—well, he wanted nothing to do with it. He knew what his experience had done to him, and he did not want to take responsibility for putting others in the same peril. Then again, there were all those millions of Chinese who had no hint of the glorious message of God's love in Christ.

Taylor's internal debates raged and raged, and during the spring of 1865 he entered in his diary, "For two or three months, intense conflict. . . . Thought I should lose my mind."[6] A friend, seeing that Taylor was torn up inside, invited him to visit Brighton on the south coast of England toward the end of June.

But torment continued. Taylor could find no rest or relaxation. On Sunday morning, as soon as the service ended, he bolted out of church. The comfortable Christianity of the church and the millions of Chinese who knew nothing of Jesus—the contrast overwhelmed him. He later recalled, "I wandered out on the sands alone, in great spiritual agony."

Sometime during that lonely walk on English shores, Taylor decided he'd had enough, that he simply couldn't deny his sense of call nor his inability to bear the crushing burden. He finally found peace when he told God that "all responsibility as to the issues and consequences must rest with him [God]; that as his servant it was mine to obey and to follow him—his to direct, to care for, and to guide me and those who might labor with me."

Some may want to argue that Taylor's torment was driven not by Jesus but by his own fears and disobedience. Perhaps. But who is it that created us in such a way that we feel a sense of torment when we refuse to do what is right? And who is it that seems not only to stick in the knife of torment but also cuts with it until the cancer of self and fear is removed from our breast?

It would be more motivating, I suppose, to be able to say that as a result of this moment, Taylor lived happily ever. In some ways, I suppose he did.

Taylor immediately wrote in his Bible: "Prayed for 24 willing, skillful laborers, Brighton, June 25/65." Within a year he had his twenty-four laborers, and together on the *Lammermuir*, they set sail for China. It was the beginning of what was to become the largest, most innovative, and most culturally sensitive missionary society in China in the nineteenth century.[7]

This was also, however, the society that had more missionaries than any others slaughtered in the Boxer Uprising thirty-five years later. And Taylor, it should be noted, suffered bouts of depression his entire life.

It would be more motivating if I could tell you that my friend kicked his pornographic habit and lived lust-free ever after. Not quite. My friend did eventually move from rationalizing his behavior to recognizing that this is a struggle he will have the rest of his life. But now he sees it as a struggle, the ebb and flow of letting Jesus deeper and deeper into his life. There are moments when he's "tormented" by Jesus because Jesus wants to destroy some unclean part of his life. Yet in those same moments, my friend wants to run ever more deeply into Jesus's presence, precisely because Jesus is able to destroy that which is unclean in him.

"In the beginning, there are a great many battles and a good deal of suffering for those who are advancing towards God," writes the desert mother known as Amma Syncletica, "and afterwards, ineffable joy. It is like those who wish to light a fire; at first they are choked by the smoke and cry, and by this means obtain what they seek—as it is said, 'Our God is a consuming fire' [Heb. 12:29]—so we also must kindle the divine fire in ourselves through tears and hard work."[8]

So many moments in the Christian life are very much like a great battle, and yet we push forward. We are up to our knees in water, and we can hear a kind of buzzing sound all around, as well as the sound of machine guns.

"Come on! Come on!" someone yells.

"I'm coming! I'm coming!" we yell back.

CHAPTER 4
Prayer
Scandals

And Simon and his companions hunted for him. When they found him, they said to him, "Everyone is searching for you." He answered, "Let us go on to the neighboring towns, so that I may proclaim the message there also; for that is what I came out to do." And he went throughout Galilee, proclaiming the message in their synagogues and casting out demons.

Mark 1:36–39

Almighty and eternal God, so draw our hearts to you, so guide our minds, so fill our imaginations, so control our wills, that we may be wholly yours, utterly dedicated to you; and then use us, we pray, as you will, and always to your glory and the welfare of your people; through our Lord and Savior Jesus Christ. Amen.

The Book of Common Prayer[1]

Prayer, when practiced with utmost attention, does strange things to people because deep prayer is nothing less than an encounter with the living God. Such an encounter prompts an aged Middle Eastern nomad named Abram to abandon his homeland. It gives a diminutive shepherd named David the wisdom and courage to lead a nation. It so humbles an angry cult-watcher named Saul that he turns his life around. It prompts a spoiled young man from Assisi to abandon the glories of a military and commercial life to live as literally as possible by the Sermon on the Mount. It inspires a young Albanian to give her life feeding those dying on the streets of Calcutta.

This divine encounter is devastating, and like a hit of spiritual heroin, the person becomes addicted to things divine, desperate for the good, the true, and the beautiful. Thus, in the Psalms, where the passions of the godly are most vividly expressed, we find a God-obsession: "Whom have I in heaven but you? And there is nothing on earth that I desire other than you" (Ps. 73:25), and "My soul is consumed with longing for your ordinances at all times. . . . With open mouth I pant . . . for your commandments" (Ps. 119:20, 131). Metaphors of thirsting and starving abound: "As a deer longs for flowing streams, so my soul longs for you, O God. My soul thirsts for God, for the living God" (Ps. 42:1–2).

So fixated are they, the God-driven cannot snap out of it even when they want to. Jeremiah writes: "If I say, 'I will not mention him, or speak any more of his name, then within me there is something like a burning fire shut up in my bones; I am weary of holding it in, and I cannot'" (Jer. 20:9).

When Francis of Assisi was attending worship one day, the Gospel lesson was from Matthew: "Do not take along any gold or silver or copper in your belts; take no bag for the journey, or extra tunic, or sandals or a staff" (Matt. 10:9–10 NIV). Francis was startled by the reading and suddenly filled with inexplicable joy: "This is what I want!" he shouted. "This is what I long for with all my heart!"[2]

"He immediately took off his shoes from his feet," Saint Bonaventure, his biographer, notes, "put aside his staff, cast away his wallet and money as if accursed, was content with one tunic and exchanged his leather belt for a piece of rope. He directed his heart's desire to carry out what he had heard and to conform in every way to the rule of right living given to the apostles."

The command of God was for Francis his joy. So it is with all the godly: there is no difference between God's commands and his rewards. God is alpha and omega, all in all, and they cannot get enough of him. They are God-addicted, like Julian of Norwich: "I saw him and sought him! I had him yet I wanted him."[3]

With heart, soul, mind, and strength completely consumed with God, the world loses many of its hues for the saint. Things moral and spiritual are seen with startling clarity and usually in black and white. You are either for God or against him; for joy or for despair; for goodness or for evil. You are willing to leave everything and anyone to follow him.

Mark reminds us in his first chapter that Jesus, too, was a man of prayer: "In the morning, while it was still very dark, he got up and went out to a deserted place, and there he prayed" (Mark 1:35). This characteristic of our Lord is noted in all the Gospels, especially Luke. Luke records not only this incident, but he also tells his readers that Jesus prayed before his baptism (Luke 3:21) and spent the night in prayer before selecting the Twelve (6:12–16). When Luke notes that Jesus "would withdraw to deserted places and pray" (Luke 5:16), he's indicating that this was a regular practice of our Lord.

It should not surprise us then that Jesus, a man of prayer even more so than the saints, will act oddly sometimes.

What Jesus does in this early scene in Mark (1:36–39) is odd indeed. Suffering people are coming to him, people who are ill, lonely, lost, crippled, anxious; some are no doubt dying. These sufferers—locals, thus many of whom he knows—are literally begging for his healing touch and life-giving words. So Simon and company search out Jesus to alert him.

Jesus just tells them to take a hike. Or more accurately, he takes a hike to go to neighboring towns, "so that" he tells them, "I may proclaim the message there also" (Mark 1:38).

In a culture in which family and community had the right to one's allegiance, this must have been something of a shock. This backwater area of the Roman Empire finally has a wonder-worker in their midst, and he's not even going to help the hometown folks? What an ingrate.

It is a strange thing to do, especially after spending an entire evening in prayer. One would assume that prayer would have made Jesus even more compassionate. Instead, after prayer, he appears more insensitive than ever.

Since we know the end of the gospel story, we can safely assume that Jesus is anything but an ingrate. We can also assume he deeply loves his family, friends, and the people who are clamoring for his help—many of whom he has known growing up in the region. He surely looks upon these people with more warmth than on a city of strangers many miles away, when he later says, "Jerusalem, Jerusalem. . . . How often have I desired to gather your children together as a hen gathers her brood under her wings" (Matt. 23:37).

We can surmise, then, that it was not an easy thing for Jesus to say to his disciples, "Let us go on to the neighboring towns" (Mark 1:38). I dare say it may have torn him apart inside.

Greater love has no man than that he should give his life for his friends, Jesus once said (see John 15:13). True enough. But it appears also to be true that sometimes no greater love has a God-lover than that he should abandon his friends, not to mention his family.

In September 1807 a self-taught twenty-five-year-old Robert Morrison landed in the Chinese port of Canton. He had come to bring the gospel to the Chinese, the first Protestant to attempt to do so. By the time he died in China twenty-seven years later, however, he had baptized only ten Chinese. History has judged, however, that Morrison was anything but a failure.

During Morrison's twenty-seven years in China, he translated hymns and prayer books into Chinese, compiled a Chinese grammar and a six-volume Chinese dictionary, and often acted as a translator for the British diplomatic corp. Along the way, Morrison was hailed for his pioneering translation work and was presented with an honorary Doctor of Divinity degree from Glasgow University and membership into the esteemed Royal Society of Science.

Morrison's greatest achievement, of course, was his translation of the Bible into Chinese, and it was this that laid the groundwork for all later missionary work. That missionary work grew slowly over the next century and a half, until the missionaries were expelled by the Chinese government in the 1950s. Since that time the Protestant church (registered and underground) has exploded, with estimates ranging from 15 to 50 million adherents.

I have visited Protestant congregations in China, and in many churches I visited, someone would point to Morrison as a spiritual father. These Christians recognize that the missionary movement was part and parcel of the oppressive colonialism of the nineteenth century. But they also refuse to denigrate the pioneering, sacrificial efforts of Morrison and others. Without him, one Chinese Christian told me, he would not know Jesus today.

Yet Morrison's legacy—and world history—would have been startlingly different if he had listened to the desperate pleas of his family just a few years before he arrived in Canton. As a young man, Morrison had become fascinated with the idea of serving Christ overseas—much to his mother's chagrin. His sense of call became so fixed that his mother felt she had to do something. So she extracted a promise from him that he would not go abroad while she was still alive—a promise he painfully made and dutifully kept. But as soon as she died, he made plans to begin his ministerial studies in earnest. He was in his early twenties, and typical of men that age, he likely felt that much of life had already passed him by. It was time to get going.

Morrison had just settled into studies at the Hoxton Academy when a letter arrived from his family. His father's health had taken a turn for the worse. Morrison's brothers, sisters, and father pleaded with him to return home.

The pressure must have been enormous. There was his sense of familial duty, which Morrison had already proved was no mere abstract ethic to him. He surely loved his father and no doubt felt sorry for his siblings. But then there was this sense of call, this inner urging to go on to other lands to proclaim the message there also, for after years of prayer, he was sure that was what he was called to do.

So no doubt with a heavy heart but a firm will, he wrote back,

> Honored father, brother, and sisters . . . the account of my father's leg growing worse and worse concerns me; but what can I do? I look to my God and my father's God. . . . You advise me to return home. I thank you for your kind intentions; may the Lord bless you for them. But I have no inclination to do so; having set my hand to the plough, I would not look back. It hath pleased the Lord to prosper me so far, and grant me favor in the eyes of this people.[4]

The history of the church is filled with similar examples. Antony of Egypt was responsible for the care of his sister after the death of their parents. Yet after he sensed a call to a life of prayer in the desert, he had to leave her in the care of others. Francis of Assisi essentially repudiated his natural father to, as he put it, give his life to his Father in heaven. Family and friends have a way of making demands on us—sometimes demands based on very real needs—but the urging of God gives us the courage to make the painful choice of ignoring those needs for another call.

But don't we also know of too many instances when this divine call was used to evade genuine responsibilities? David Livingstone left his wife and family in England for years at a time so that he could sojourn in Africa. John Wesley and George Whitfield abandoned their wives for months at a time to preach in England and America. And how many children of pastors, filled with resentment, refuse to darken the door of a church today because to them "the call of God" was nothing but an excuse for their parents to ignore them and indulge in their religious enthusiasms?

So we find that this little story in Mark has a double edge. How simple it would be to end this chapter with a bold call to leave family and friends to follow the upward call of God. Or how easy it would be to simply scold religious enthusiasts for ignoring their familial duty.

But Jesus won't let us off the hook so easily. The Jesus who in this passage leaves family and friends to preach and heal relative strangers is the same one who stayed at home until he was thirty, long past the age when young men of that day did so.

It seems that there is a time to do one's familial duty, to stay with the mother who insists on it, perhaps even to her death. And there is a time to ignore the pleas of family and friends, even when those pleas arise out of genuine need.

Ah, but how do we know which time is which? Perhaps there are guidelines or principles that tell us what to do, when to nurture family and when to minister to the stranger. Perhaps there is an aphorism that can give us wisdom or a wise man who can teach us the inerrant way. No, the solid guidance we need is found elsewhere, in a place more mysterious.

It is the place where Jesus went time and again, the place that let him know when it was time to stay in Nazareth and when it was time to move on to other regions. It is the place where Morrison and Antony and Francis and others learned when to love their families and when to love the lost. It is the place where we encounter the living God.

Prayer is a mysterious, unfathomable, intense conversation with the Father, who will not give us formulas and principles but will give us himself. The guidance he gives, of course, does not come in an instant, and it does not come as clearly as an email. But come it will for those who, like Jesus and the saints, seek out this place regularly.

And though this little story does not guide us in all our decisions, it does point to one reality of the disciple's life. Deep and ongoing prayer will sometimes prompt us to do seemingly scandalous things. That means sometimes we may even do things that will confuse our loved ones and fill us with heartache. But in the end, what choice does a disciple have? Like Jeremiah, our hearts burn within. We simply have to go on to the neighboring towns so that we may proclaim the message there also; for that is what we are called to do.

CHAPTER 5
It's Not Nice to Be Nice

A leper came to him begging him, and kneeling he said to him, "If you choose, you can make me clean." Moved with pity, Jesus stretched out his hand and touched him, and said to him, "I do choose. Be made clean!" Immediately the leprosy left him, and he was made clean. After sternly warning him he sent him away at once.

Mark 1:40–43

In our discipline, the question is not whether the devout soul is angry. . . . To be indignant with a sinner with a view to his correction . . . as far as I can see, no sane judgment could reprove.

Augustine[1]

On All Saints Day many congregations sing a hymn that begins, "I sing a song of the saints of God, patient and brave and true."[2] Though principalities threaten and rage, saints do their duty. This usually amounts to telling the truth, and that, in turn, usually results in their being jailed, beaten, burned, or beheaded. Saints are brave and true indeed.

But patient? The word conjures up haloed saints listening sensitively to others' worries, smiling at people's weaknesses, and setting sinners back on the path of virtue with a gentle pat on the back. Surely saints were nice people—that's why they're called *saints*. That's why we say a forbearing person is "patient as a saint."

But saints, it turns out, are not all that patient. Or forbearing. Or nice. The lives of Athanasius, Jerome, Francis, Luther, and Theresa of Avila, just to name a few, are littered with examples of impatience.

Take Saint Catherine of Siena, one of the most extraordinary women of the fourteenth century. From her earliest childhood, she saw visions and practiced extreme spiritual disciplines. At age sixteen she joined the lay branch of the Dominicans and later underwent a profound mystical experience. She cared for the sick, dressing and serving lepers and others with hideous skin cancers.

In Catherine's *Dialogues*, through the voice of her "Eternal Father," she teaches such things as, "By humbling yourself in the valley of humility, you will know Me and yourself, from which knowledge you will draw all that is necessary," and "Every perfection and every virtue proceeds from charity, and charity is nourished by humility."[3] Her teachings on the spiritual life are so saintly and influential that the Roman Catholic Church made her a doctor of the church in 1970.

This same Catherine once went to Avignon, France, to meet Pope Gregory XI. This was an exceptional occasion for a medieval Christian, and most would have felt a sense of awe when entering the pope's presence and would have nervously rehearsed some humble act of deference to greet him.

Not Catherine. When she met the Vicar of Christ, she blurted out that in the very place where all heavenly virtues should flourish, she only smelled the stink of hell's putrefaction.

Catherine was referring to the glittering pomp of the Avignon papacy, where church offices were sold to the highest bidder and pope, cardinals, and bishops sported silk and jewels, and their houses were trimmed with gold and ivory. Meanwhile the threadbare clothing, crumbling shelters, and malnourished bodies of Christians across Europe went unnoticed by the papal bureaucrats. Catherine thought she would remind the pope, not so gently, of the contrast.

The pope, a man not easily intimidated, wryly asked how Catherine, a recent visitor to Avignon, could possibly know about his odor: "How have you, who have been here such a short time, got such knowledge of all that goes on here?"[4]

Catherine didn't miss a beat. She replied that she had smelled the stench while she was still in Siena, some four hundred miles away. "I smelt the stink of the sins which flourish in the papal court while I was still at home."

Rude. Uncivil. Sarcastic. And, it turns out, saintly.

Jesus opens his ministry as a rather exacting rabbi. He suddenly appears before two groups of fishermen and starkly commands them, "Follow me!" (Mark 1:16–20). He tells a deranged man to shut up and then causes him to writhe in pain (Mark 1:25–26). After Jesus heals a helpless leper, Mark says, "sternly warning him, [Jesus] sent him away at once" (Mark 1:43).

The Greek behind the phrase "sternly warning him" can mean "to denounce harshly, to scold." And the phrase, "he sent him away at once" is a translation of the Greek verb *ekballō*, which elsewhere is translated "to drive out," and "to throw out." A plain reading of the passage suggests that Jesus scolds the man and then throws him out. It is no wonder that some ancient manuscripts read that at the opening of this incident Jesus, after being interrupted by this leper, is moved not with "pity" but with "anger." That reading at least accords with Jesus's overall demeanor here.

This is not unusual behavior for our Messiah. Jesus throws people out of a room (*ekballō* again) so he can heal a child, and then he "strictly ordered" witnesses of the miracle to keep quiet (Mark 5:40, 43). He and Peter get into a row, each rebuking the other (Mark 8:32–33). Jesus becomes exasperated with a crowd and his disciples: "You faithless generation, how much longer must I be among you? How much longer must I put up with you?" (Mark 9:19). He curses a fig tree (Mark 11:13–14). He drives people out of the temple area (with a whip, according to John 2:15), overturning tables, and physically intimidating people to prevent their passing through (Mark 11:15–17).

Jesus's attitude toward authorities is hardly respectful. He calls Herod a fox (Luke 13:32), and he castigates the scribes and Pharisees at length, mocking them as "blind guides" and "hypocrites" (Matt. 23:24–25), and practically curses them, saying, "You are like whitewashed tombs, which on the outside look beautiful, but inside they are full of the bones of the dead and of all kinds of filth" (Matt. 23:27).

Such incidents crop up again and again in the Jesus story. That story, in fact, is inexplicable without them. If Jesus was merely loving, compassionate, and kind—if Jesus was only nice—why did both Jews and Romans feel compelled to murder him?

Naturally enough, these are not passages upon which we meditate in morning devotions, nor do we memorize them for inspiration. Why bother when, if we just keep reading, we'll find something edifying? And so, despite their prominence in the Gospels, these passages remain foreign to us. And there's a reason for that.

Today we are adherents of the Religion of Niceness. In this religion, God is a benevolent grandfather who winks at human mistakes, and it goes without saying that he always understands—after all, it is human to err, divine to forgive.

Christians are often fascinated with the Religion of Niceness because it appears to champion biblical virtues such as humility, forgiveness, and mercy. This religion so permeates our consciousness that when we hear someone quote the second Great Commandment, the epitome of Christian ethics, we tend to hear: "Be nice to your neighbor, as you would have your neighbor be nice to you."

I indoctrinated my children into this faith from their earliest days. My five-year-old son's friend visits our home. This friend grabs one of my son's toys, and my son comes running to me, complaining about his friend's selfishness. I tell him not to make a fuss, to share his toys, to be nice.

Days later, I arrange for my son to visit that friend's house while I spend time with the parents. This time, the friend refuses to let my son play with one of his toys; my son comes running to me and complains about his friend's selfishness. I tell him that since we are guests, he should be nice and not make a fuss.

Lesson: it's not about what's right; it's about avoiding conflict. The last thing the busy parent wants to do in this situation is mete out justice, confront selfishness (especially in someone else's child), or ask another parent to teach his or her kid some manners. Better to fall back on admonitions to be nice.

Thus we learn not to make a fuss in school, at work, in life. We quickly discover that people respond positively to us when we are nice to them and negatively when we aren't. Since it feels good to be liked, we get addicted to being nice. And this addiction skews our reasoning. We imagine that if someone makes us feel good (by being nice to us), she is being loving, and if she makes us feel bad (by being stern), she doesn't like us. We have powerful social and psychological forces that keep reinforcing the ethic of niceness.

For a couple of years, we had a black teenager living with us. Having been deserted by his father at a young age, he was anxious to form bonds with older men, including coaches. Consequently, he was affable, eager to please, and respectful of authority. He never questioned a coach's decision, at least not to his face.

Once when he complained to me that his coach wasn't giving him enough playing time, I asked him, "Have you asked your coach why?"

"That would be disrespectful," he said.

"It's not disrespectful to ask questions," I replied.

"But it would be like I was challenging his authority, questioning his judgment."

"Not if you did it with the right spirit."

"It doesn't matter how you do it; it's disrespectful."

And around we went. By being nice, he was avoiding all sorts of uncomfortable emotions. This young man had unique issues, of course, but not so unique that most of us can't identify with him. We all have people with whom we sacrifice truthfulness on the altar of niceness. The difference between my foster son and those reading (and the one writing) this book is this: he had no idea that his behavior was harming his ability to form deeper relationships—ones characterized by honesty and freedom. But I know this behavior tends to undermine my relationships, and yet I fall into it time and again.

This ethic of niceness can have disastrous consequences for the church as well. I once was a part of an Episcopalian parish that, despite fierce debate at the national level, managed to keep the issues of homosexuality and biblical interpretation under wraps at the congregational level. Our unspoken motto was, "Let's just agree to disagree and go about our life together." This was despite the fact that it was increasingly clear that there was no way to agree to disagree for very long on such fundamental matters.

When the denomination installed a noncelibate homosexual as a bishop in the fall of 2003, we could no longer avoid talking about these matters. We were shocked to discover that we had two different congregations—with radically different assumptions about the most basic things. Since we had no track record of speaking the truth in love to one another, we found ourselves shouting at each other. It was, to say the least, extremely painful, and it wasn't long before the church divided.

Better to have addressed these issues years earlier in a frank and charitable manner—even though raising such issues would have broken the code of Episcopal decorum. An earlier conversation would have left some feeling alienated, and some would have left. But that would have been preferable to the congregation literally splitting in two later on.

In her essay "Nice Is Not the Point," Marilyn Chandler McEntyre writes, "One of my husband's finer moments in parenting came one day when, after he had uttered an unwelcome word of correction to a disgruntled child, he leaned down, looked her in the eye, and said, 'Honey, this is what love looks like.' Love, in that case, must have seemed to her a far cry from nice."[5]

When Jesus speaks sternly to the healed leper, when he castigates the Pharisees, when he rebukes Peter, it seems like a far cry from nice. But it isn't a far cry from love. Simply put, when Jesus is not nice, he's trying to get people to do the right thing.

Take the healed leper. The context of Jesus' sternness is quickly made clear: "After sternly warning him he sent him away at once, saying to him, 'See that you say nothing to anyone; but go, show yourself to the priest, and offer for your cleansing what Moses commanded, as a testimony to them.' But he went out and began to proclaim it freely, and to spread the word, so that Jesus could no longer go into a town openly, but stayed out in the country; and people came to him from every quarter" (Mark 1:43–45).

Jesus realizes that the leper is grateful and that he wants to do something extraordinary for Jesus. But Jesus does not want the extraordinary. He wants the man to do what the day's religious conventions (as outlined in Leviticus 14) told him to do. If the man really wanted to do something for Jesus, he would have played it by the book. This would have demonstrated to the authorities that Jesus was no law breaker (an accusation he knew he'd have to confront sooner or later), and this would have allowed Jesus to continue his ministry in towns throughout Galilee.

As commentator Ben Witherington puts it, the man healed of leprosy "bore witness about the wrong thing in the wrong way."[6] Thus Jesus could no longer enter towns and therefore synagogues—houses of worship and education, the richly symbolic place where he would have preferred to speak about the fulfillment of Israel. Now people began to mob him, not to hear his message so much as to be healed of their infirmities.

Variations of this theme—Jesus wanting others to do the right thing—are seen in Jesus's rebuke of the Pharisees' hypocrisy and Peter's ignorance. Jesus is less than nice because people are often wicked and foolish, and they need to be jolted out of their stupor. Simply put: "The Lord disciplines those whom he loves" (Heb. 12:6).

Such confrontation is more than helping people do the right thing. It's also about deepening our relationships with one another. Thus Paul tells the church in Colossae, "Let the word of Christ dwell in you richly; teach and admonish one another in all wisdom" (Col. 3:16), in the same passage in which he urges them, "Clothe yourselves with love, which binds everything together in perfect harmony" (Col. 3:14). There is a deeper unity, an intimacy that Paul longs for in the church, and that intimacy is brought about by a variety of behaviors such as "compassion, kindness, humility, meekness, and patience" (Col. 3:12) but also by the courage to "admonish one another."

Married couples know when their relationship moves into a deeper intimacy: it's when they start arguing regularly. Indeed, many arguments have nothing to do with love, but a lot of them do. They often begin when one spouse has the uncomfortable duty of telling the other spouse, "You have done something wrong."

This can be said in the nicest tone, but it rarely feels nice hearing it. And so it usually leads to a "conversation" that becomes less than nice. The spouse who starts this whole thing has to have a lot of courage, which is why most couples don't do it until they are some distance into the relationship, when they are pretty sure the other is not going to walk out on them. They are willing to risk arguments because they know that unless the relationship moves into the not-nice stage, their love will never deepen.

We still balk, of course. Jesus could get away with this sort of thing because he was perfect, as could Paul, we think, because he was inspired, as could the saints because they were holy. We are anything but perfect, inspired, or holy. What right have we to confront anyone else? Did not Jesus teach, "Do not judge, so that you may not be judged" (Matt. 7:1)?

This natural reticence is praiseworthy, for the hair-trigger personality that lashes out at every sign of sinfulness is one easily seduced by hypocrisy. But while all this seems humble and loving, in the end it is neither. It is not humble because it is a direct refusal to live like Jesus or to do what Jesus tells us to do: "If another member of the church sins against you," he says, "go and point out the fault when the two of you are alone" (Matt. 18:15).

Many early manuscripts of this passage read simply, "If another member of the church sins, go and . . ." This suggests that the earliest Christians believed that Jesus was not talking only about interpersonal conflict but immorality in general. As Paul puts in his letter to the Christians in Galatia: "My friends, if anyone is detected in a transgression, you who have received the Spirit should restore such a one in a spirit of gentleness" (Gal. 6:1).

Paul's words remind us that our confrontation with wrongdoing should usually be done in a "spirit of gentleness." The New Testament is not encouraging us to become hotheads. But the example of Jesus and Paul and the saints suggests that sometimes brusque confrontation is necessary. To avoid it is essentially to say that Jesus got this wrong. And to refuse confrontation is also to refuse to love.

One semester in college, I shared a house with three friends. We took turns cooking, and whenever it was my turn, I would open a can of whatever, heat it, and dish it out. By contrast, my friends often prepared thoughtful and balanced dinners. When the three of them saw an unhealthy pattern developing, they sat me down at the kitchen table and told me they didn't think I was doing my part.

I remember sitting there under their glare and that of the kitchen lights, feeling both guilty and defensive. It is still painful as I recall it over thirty years later. But I remain thankful they told me.

Had my friends decided to be nice because, after all, they were hardly perfect roommates in other respects, they would have left me wallowing in my sloth and self-centeredness. Instead their love for me was deeper than their shame at their own shortcomings. And as a result, I learned to make pretty good spaghetti.

Two qualifications are in order. First, most circumstances call us to be civil, courteous, patient—nice. We're not going to get much of a hearing for the Good News if we are regularly rude and uncivil. While we need some prophetic, even angry, voices to remind us of sin and injustice sometimes, we also need those who call for civil and patient conversation. Niceness may not be a synonym for love, but it is the usual (if not the only) way that love is expressed.

In addition, we must note that more is at stake than behavior modification. In Jesus's case, sometimes his anger actually does not make any practical difference. The leper still went out and blabbed about his healing. The Pharisees continued to be hypocrites. Peter, at least until the resurrection, continued to imagine that Jesus was a political Messiah—when Jesus was arrested, Peter even assaulted one of the guards.

The point is not that in order to be effective, one has to get a little angry once in a while. That is true as far as it goes, as any parent, teacher, coach, or spouse will attest. We don't need biblical revelation to teach us that. Jesus was a sharp judge of character, and he employed anger even when he was aware it wasn't going to do any good. Why? Because sometimes the most honest and truthful response to foolishness or evil is anger. Jesus couldn't have integrity if he was indifferent. The person who is always nice, always decorous, always even-keeled is likely a person who ultimately does not care about what God cares about.

Writer Eugene Peterson puts it this way: "It is in the things that we care about that we are capable of expressing anger. A parent sees a child dart out into a roadway and narrowly miss being hit by a car, and angrily yells at the child, at the driver—at both." The anger, he concludes, is evidence of concern: "Indifference would be somehow inhuman."[7]

Scholar Ben Witherington furthers the point: "One could even say that righteous anger is a prerequisite of ministry, for a person who has no capacity for righteous anger at the things that destroy humankind is a person who fails to be truly compassionate."[8]

If God as revealed in Jesus Christ is sometimes a jealous and angry deity, so will his disciples be—jealous for holiness, angry with foolishness. And sometimes just plain not nice.

CHAPTER 6
Love That Makes Enemies

He looked around at them with anger; he was grieved at their hardness of heart and said to the man, "Stretch out your hand." He stretched it out, and his hand was restored. The Pharisees went out and immediately conspired with the Herodians against him, how to destroy him.

Mark 3:5–6

I never gave them hell. I just tell the truth, and they think it is hell.

Harry S. Truman[1]

"Golden Mouth" was the greatest preacher of his era—the fourth century—and one of the greatest preachers in the history of the church. And yet we hardly know of him.

John Chrysostom is what we call him today. The name "Golden Mouth" was given to him long after his death because at his death not many thought he was golden. He died in exile, rejected by the powers that be, the very powers that had courted him and that had such hope for him.

Chrysostom got his start in Antioch, the city where a couple of centuries earlier the followers of Jesus were first called "Christians" (Acts 11:26). In Chrysostom's day it was a major city in the Roman Empire, and there he served as a deacon and then as a priest at the behest of the bishop. Upon occasion Chrysostom preached, and it wasn't long before his reputation for eloquence spread—especially due to the sermons he preached in the aftermath of severe riots that had erupted in Antioch in AD 387.

Soon Chrysostom's name was being whispered in the capital, Constantinople, and when the bishop there died, the imperial family decided they wanted nothing but the best for their basilica. So they kidnapped Chrysostom, dragged him to Constantinople, and consecrated him as the new bishop. A fervent believer in God's providence, Chrysostom took it as God's will and agreed to serve—a decision the imperial family would eventually regret.

Chrysostom was scandalized by the worldliness that had infected the Christian church in the capital. It was an affront to the name of God. It was a scandal in the midst of so much poverty. So, for the love of God and neighbor, he began, in the words of the ancient historian Palladius, "sweeping the stairs from the top." He reduced the expenses of his household and put an end to the frequent and extravagant banquets. (From the money he saved in the first year alone, he built a clinic for the poor.) He insisted that his clergy be above suspicion, so he forbade them an accustomed practice, which was causing no shortage of rumors: keeping in their homes women housekeepers who had vowed virginity. He also defrocked two deacons, one for murder and the other for adultery. And he insisted that monks no longer wander about at will but be attached to the discipline of a monastery.

Chrysostom also turned his attention to his flock, which included the imperial family. He was genuinely concerned for the state of their souls. So he frequently preached against the extravagances of the rich, and especially the vanity of women who spent all their time anxious about the latest fashions. While the common people were delighted with such preaching, the elite increasingly squirmed—especially when he accused leading officials of injustice (for example, depriving a widow of her inheritance).

The politics of the day were truly Byzantine and much too complicated to go into here. Suffice it to say that Chrysostom's continued outspokenness made it easier and easier for authorities to trump up reasons to get rid of him. After one aborted attempt, Chrysostom was finally seized and sent into exile. The imperial authorities did not have the courage simply to kill him but instead made him endure forced marches in the harsh climate of northern Armenia, where he finally collapsed and died.[2]

Faithful Christians will be persecuted. I was taught this axiom as a boy when I attended a fundamentalist church. It was bracing, and it emboldened us to stand by our convictions. As abolitionist Charles Finney puts it, "The inherent antagonism existing between the friends and the enemies of God renders this forever certain. . . . Such is the nature of holiness, the antagonism between them is irreconcilable. Hence, righteous men will array opposition against themselves."[3]

As I got older, however, this axiom was hardly ever heard, whether I attended mainline or evangelical churches. We were to emphasize love, thus many churches saw their business as trying to identify with the surrounding culture in an effort (at least originally) to reach more people for Christ. At the same time, I began to see that many of my fundamentalist friends didn't take as much delight in loving as in antagonizing their neighbors. The measure of faithfulness to them was not love but rejection. This struck me as perverse, and as the years went on, I tended to buy into the new model.

As I've gotten older, I've come more and more to think that despite their various extremisms, my fundamentalist friends may be right in one respect. I still think they are mistaken about what many consider core issues of the times—evolution, alcohol, and R-rated movies. But their basic instincts are profoundly Christlike: if we're not offending some people, we're likely not loving people as Christ would love them.

I've come to this conclusion after studying the lives of saints such as John Chrysostom as well as the ministry of Jesus.

The incident in Mark 3:1–6 comes at the end of a string of confrontations, each one more dramatic than the next. It begins when Jesus forgives the sins of a paralytic—an act that shocks the scribes. "Why does this fellow speak in this way?" they wonder. "It is blasphemy!" (Mark 2:7). It continues when Jesus accepts a dinner invitation from tax collectors and sinners—outcasts of the day. The Pharisees carp at his disciples, "Why does he eat with tax collectors and sinners?" (2:16). It escalates to the point where the Pharisees finally have the nerve to confront Jesus directly. After watching his disciples pluck heads of grain on the Sabbath, they interrogate him: "Look, why are they doing what is not lawful on the sabbath?" (2:24).

Now the incident. It is the Sabbath again. A man with a withered hand stands before Jesus. The Pharisees have had enough and are looking for a misstep on Jesus's part. "They watched him to see whether he would cure on the sabbath, so that they might accuse him" (3:2).

If Jesus had taken a few classes in conflict management, he would have known how to defuse the situation. He doesn't have to heal this man at that moment. If he could wait just a few hours until the sun sets and the Sabbath is over, all will be well. Instead, he challenges the Pharisees in front of the crowd.

He brings the man to the middle of the room and then turns and challenges the Pharisees with, "Is it lawful to do good or to do harm on the sabbath, to save life or to kill?" (3:4).

In fact, no Pharisee considered it unlawful to save a life on the Sabbath, and no one's life was being threatened here. As New Testament scholar Joel Marcus puts it, "Jesus makes withholding the cure of the man's paralyzed hand, even for a few hours, tantamount to killing him, and performing the cure immediately tantamount to saving his life."[4] Jesus is needlessly provoking the situation.

When the Pharisees refuse to answer him, Jesus's patience runs out: "He looked around at them with anger" (3:5). It is clearly a righteous anger, but it is an anger grounded in grief. Later when he reflects on the inability of his people to trust him, Jesus cries out, "Jerusalem, Jerusalem, the city that kills the prophets and stones those who are sent to it! How often have I desired to gather your children together as a hen gathers her brood under her wings, and you were not willing!" (Matt. 23:37).

Jesus provokes the Pharisees not because he is a trouble-maker but because he is a lover. Yes, of even the Pharisees. And he judges that at this point in his ministry, the clearest, cleanest way to tell them they have strayed far from the ways of God is to confront them publicly.

It is a love mixed with courage because Jesus knows it will bring him trouble. The combination of breaking the Sabbath and public provocation infuriates the Pharisees so much that they conspire with political enemies, the Herodians, to figure out how to get rid of Jesus. This was a remarkable moment. Herodians were Jews who supported King Herod, Rome's representative in Israel. The Pharisees would have judged the Herodians as traitors to Israel and apostates of Jewish faith. That they would conspire with their political and religious enemies says how much they despised their new, and common, enemy.

That's the problem when you mix love and courage.

This incident in Mark 3 is a particularly dramatic example of how the love of God and neighbor makes enemies. But we need to understand how common this relationship is. Let me risk belaboring the point by showing what a regular feature it is in the Gospels and the rest of the New Testament. It's a relationship woven into the very fabric of discipleship.

For example, Jesus concludes the Beatitudes in this way: "Blessed are those who are persecuted for righteousness' sake, for theirs is the kingdom of heaven." And to make sure his disciples get the point, he punctuates this last beatitude, by repeating it in stronger language: "Blessed are you when people revile you and persecute you and utter all kinds of evil against you falsely on my account. Rejoice and be glad, for your reward is great in heaven, for in the same way they persecuted the prophets who were before you" (Matt. 5:10–11).

This is hardly the last time Jesus teaches on the topic. "But I say to you that listen, Love your enemies, do good to those who hate you, bless those who curse you, pray for those who abuse you" (Luke 6:27–28). He would not teach them about how to treat enemies unless he assumed they were going to create some.

Jesus also says, "See, I am sending you out like sheep into the midst of wolves; so be wise as serpents and innocent as doves. Beware of them, for they will hand you over to councils and flog you in their synagogues; and you will be dragged before governors and kings because of me, as a testimony to them and the Gentiles" (Matt. 10:16–18).

And Jesus says this:

I came to bring fire to the earth, and how I wish it were already kindled! I have a baptism with which to be baptized, and what stress I am under until it is completed! Do you think that I have come to bring peace to the earth? No, I tell you, but rather division! From now on five in one household will be divided, three against two and two against three; they will be divided: father against son and son against father, mother against daughter and daughter against mother, mother-in-law against her daughter-in-law and daughter-in-law against mother-in-law.

Luke 12:49–53

Other times Jesus drives home the point in counterpoint: "Woe to you when all speak well of you, for that is what their ancestors did to the false prophets" (Luke 6:26).

Jesus sounds like those crazy fundamentalists! And he's not the only one. James says the same sort of thing when he castigates fellow Christians: "Adulterers! Do you not know that friendship with the world is enmity with God? Therefore whoever wishes to be a friend of the world becomes an enemy of God" (James 4:4). And the writer of Hebrews reminds his readers, "But recall those earlier days when, after you had been enlightened, you endured a hard struggle with sufferings, sometimes being publicly exposed to abuse and persecution, and sometimes being partners with those so treated" (Heb. 10:32–33).

Paul puts it succinctly and sweepingly in his second letter to Timothy: "Indeed, all who want to live a godly life in Christ Jesus will be persecuted" (2 Tim. 3:12). For Paul and his companions, ministry is a litany of harassment and conflict with enemies. As Eugene Peterson says, "His life recklessly caromed from adversity to persecution and back to adversity."[5] A typical example: "But the Jews incited the devout women of high standing and the leading men of the city, and stirred up persecution against Paul and Barnabas, and drove them out of their region" (Acts 13:50).

So it goes in nearly every city in which Paul preached and ministered. For the sake of the cities he visited, he proclaimed the gospel of the true and living God. And that usually entailed telling people in one way or another that their idols were false, their religion incomplete at best. That sort of thing—though it needs to be done from time to time—does not go over well.

You would think speaking the truth *in love* would be enough to diffuse anger. Not necessarily.

Most people have had conversations that go something like this: A friend or pastor or teacher or someone says something that we think is patently false or harmful. We decide we cannot stay silent. So—and I'm speaking of us here in our better moments!—we write a calm, reasoned email to explain our concerns with frankness but a genuine spirit of love.

What we get back is anything but calm and reasoned. It is defensive, angry, or maybe even a curt conversation stopper that says nothing more than, "I'm sorry you're so upset." That's it.

But we're not satisfied. The friendship is too important, or the issue is too critical. So we pursue our friend, again, with patience, with tact, trying to get a conversation going.

Then comes a saucy response, full of sarcasm, long on anger and short on reason. We're taken aback. We try again to get the conversation back on an even keel so we can discuss issues, not throw darts. All to no avail. Round it goes for email after email— or conversation after conversation—until we realize that, though we have been as tactful as tactful can be, the truth has touched a raw nerve. And we fear we may have lost a friend.

Truthful confrontation is one sure way to create enemies. Just acting with compassion is another.

Jonathan Taylor, a college student from Biola University, needed to fulfill the university's ministry requirement, so he decided to choose an activity that would make him most uncomfortable—visiting an AIDS patient. He volunteered at the Carl Bean House, in South Los Angeles, and there he met Lance Loud.

As Taylor puts it, Lance had been a "writer, stripper, roadie, model, artist, rock star, band manager, television personality, and icon of gay culture." He visited Lance a couple times a week for a few months and spent most of his time listening, empathizing, and trying to understand this brash, loud, sometimes caustic gay man who was dying. Taylor talked about his faith to Lance, but mostly he lived out a ministry of kindness—like smuggling into the hospice a couple of kittens for a dying man who loved cats.[6]

Taylor described his experience for *Christianity Today*—to the dismay of many readers. While many applauded Taylor for his courage and sensitivity, many wondered why a good Christian was being so nice to a defiant homosexual. They would have been comforted, it seems, if Taylor had preached at Lance and walked away. As it was, they were uncomfortable that he tried to love Lance and spent time with him.

It is the same problem Jesus ran into when he dined with "tax collectors and sinners"—a despised group of his day: "And as he sat at dinner in Levi's house, many tax collectors and sinners were also sitting with Jesus and his disciples—for there were many who followed him. When the scribes of the Pharisees saw that he was eating with sinners and tax collectors, they said to his disciples, 'Why does he eat with tax collectors and sinners?'" (Mark 2:15–16).

If we fraternize with a perceived enemy of faith or morality, we run the risk of creating other enemies—sometimes even within the household of faith.

Fraternize is the appropriate word. It means, according to the *American Heritage Dictionary*, "To associate with others in a brotherly or congenial way," or "To associate on friendly terms with an enemy or opposing group." It comes from the Latin *fraternus*, or "brotherly." It means to treat someone who is not family—and by current standards don't deserve to be family—as if he were family. It is to hug a promiscuous homosexual. It is to have dinner with radical Muslims. It is to speak compassionately with an abortionist. It is to continue to treat with respect the liberal (or the fundamentalist).

To be sure, there is risk especially in loving the theological or morally wayward. Out of mere sympathy, we may become tempted to compromise our values to be nice to them. But true love is robust. It includes compassion *and* confrontation, empathy *and* truth-telling, kindness *and* sternness. When we enter such relationships, we must enter them not with sentimentality but with full-orbed love. This takes not only compassion but courage. Yet it is that very combination that so often gets us into trouble.

The point is not to create enemies but to be faithful to Christ in word and deed. That means mostly to speak and act in love. If in our speech or acts of love we are merely anxious to proclaim our self-righteousness—if we are proud of our truth, haughty in our love—well, we deserve to have enemies and don't deserve the name *Christian*.

But if we are sincerely trying to address important issues and do our best to present the truth in a way that we think will persuade, if we refuse to duck our responsibility to speak and to act, if we are really trying to love in word and deed—then we should brace ourselves for a fair amount of hostility. And we should prepare ourselves for the inevitable demons of doubt and sadness that will stalk us: "Is this really necessary?" "Is it really worth all this trouble?" "Do you really need to do this now?" It should never surprise us when our love for others makes them feel uncomfortable, even hostile.

In the end, the lover of truth and doer of love will sometimes, like Jesus, be both mean and wild—mean with righteous anger, and wild with inconsolable grief: "Jerusalem, Jerusalem!"

CHAPTER 7
Wretched Individualism

Then his mother and his brothers came; and standing outside, they sent to him and called him. A crowd was sitting around him; and they said to him, "Your mother and your brothers and sisters are outside, asking for you." And he replied, "Who are my mother and my brothers?" And looking at those who sat around him, he said, "Here are my mother and my brothers! Whoever does the will of God is my brother and sister and mother."

Mark 3:31–35

Even cursory glances through the Gospels confirm that the work Jesus did in the lives of his disciples occurred because the disciples were in relationship, not simply with him, but with one another.

Richard Lamb[1]

In this passage, the "mean" Jesus challenges one of the most powerful and pervasive of American myths. Given that we are so immersed in this culture, it is nearly impossible for us to see it because on the surface he appears to reinforce the myth. So we are going to have to do some mental work to step outside the familiar so we can see the familiar afresh.

One way to do that is to transport ourselves to an era that seems utterly unlike ours, to rehearse one of the most famous stories in Christian history that seems, on the surface, also to reinforce this American myth. But just as visiting another culture gives insights into your own, so spending some time in the past can give us insights into the challenges of the twenty-first century.

Peter Bernadone, father of Francis of Assisi, though not as greedy as some historians have made him out, was nonetheless ambitious for wealth and prestige. And what he wanted for himself, he wanted even more for his children.

Bernadone was in the cloth business. Because he found Italian wools too coarse, he often traveled to fairs in Provence and Champagne, where he could procure the finest materials then available. He likely took his sons, Francis and Angelo, with him on such trips to let them experience something of the larger world and to teach them the business.

Francis learned the business well. Growing up, he waited on customers and rode on horseback to nearby towns to sell goods, so that after a few years, as one biographer puts it, he had become "most prudent in business." A man after his father's heart.

Though prudent on the income side of the ledger, Francis was anything but that on the expense side. One of his biographers says, "He was most lavish in spending, so much so that all he could possess and earn was squandered on feasting and other pursuits . . . spending more money on expensive clothes than his social position warranted."[2]

Yet as he moved into his early twenties, Francis became increasingly dissatisfied with his life. Business did not capture his imagination, and hedonism did not capture his heart.

One evening friends arrived at Francis's home in mirthful spirits. They handed him a mock scepter and proclaimed him "king of youth." They wanted him to lead them through the streets of Assisi in a drinking and singing fest—and for Francis to foot the bill, as he usually did. Francis obliged, and the rambunctious group wandered out, increasingly drunk and raucous as the evening wore on.

But Francis couldn't work himself up into his typical partying mood. He became increasingly reflective. Then at one point in the evening, he was inexplicably filled with a sense of warmth and peace. He groped for what it might mean.

Francis's friends had gone on ahead, but when they discovered their patron missing, they searched him out. When they found him, they sensed something amiss and jokingly asked if he was imagining what kind of woman he might marry. "You're right," he replied as if waking up. "I was thinking about taking a wife more noble, wealthier, and more beautiful than you have ever seen."

They all had a good laugh at that. But Francis was serious, as they would soon find out. At this point, however, he only had a vague sense of who this "lady" would be.

Over the next months, Francis increasingly spoke to his family and friends about the "hidden treasure" he was discovering, and he started giving more alms to beggars. If he had no money, he sometimes literally gave them the shirt off his back, or his belt, or his hat. He saved leftovers from the dinner table and distributed them to the poor.

When Francis went on a pilgrimage to Rome, he lived for a few days like the city's beggars: he stripped himself of his middle-class attire, shared their meals, and begged on the streets as they did. When he returned to Assisi, he did even more for the poor and even spent time with lepers. The town couldn't help but notice, as did his family, and people were starting to talk.

This sort of thing—scandalized talk—happens in every generation when someone decides to follow the will of God seriously. It happens even in cultures completely immersed in Christian faith, like medieval Italy. It happens even when the one living out the will of God is faultless: Jesus's friends were so troubled by his strange teachings and itinerant lifestyle, that they convinced his family "to restrain him, for people were saying, 'He has gone out of his mind'" (Mark 3:21).

The God-inspired bewilderment, and sometimes estrangement, happens in the church today, and you don't have to act as radical as Francis. My wife once had a conversation with a woman who had been a longtime member of the Episcopal church we were attending. She was telling Barbara how concerned she was for her daughter.

Her daughter was intellectually gifted and had gone to a prestigious university in the South. Sometime in college her faith had been ignited, and she turned from nominal Episcopalianism to being fervently evangelical. She began participating in Campus Crusade outreach campaigns, and then, to her parents' dismay, said she was going to the mission field.

The mother was not so much hostile to the idea as bewildered. Was this the best way for her daughter to use her intellectual gifts? Was she not squandering four years of university education? Was there really much future in this line of work?

Francis began taking long walks in the countryside to ponder what exactly God wanted of him. One day he stopped to pray in a little, dilapidated chapel, San Damiano. The walls were crumbling, and the priest eked out an existence—he didn't even have enough money to buy oil to burn on the altar.

Francis knelt in the darkened nave and gazed at the crucifix. It's unclear how long he was there, but at some point he heard Christ speak to him: "Francis, go and repair my house, which you can see, is all being destroyed." As one of his biographers puts it, Francis was "more than a little stunned," and he began "trembling and stuttering like a man out of his senses."

Francis was nothing if not concrete in his thinking, and he immediately concluded that it was *this* little church in which he was praying that needed rebuilding. At the same time, his business training kicked in: he started mentally calculating the materials, tools, and capital he needed to get started.

In short order Francis made his way back to Assisi and went to his father's shop. He gathered up a variety of fabrics (especially scarlet, which would fetch a good price), mounted the family horse, and set off for nearby Foligno and the market there. He quickly found buyers for the cloth, and then he decided to sell the family horse as well! Francis then returned to San Damiano, proudly showed the priest what he had done, and began buying supplies and started rebuilding.

It didn't take long for the frugal Peter Bernadone to see that some of his inventory was missing, not to mention the family horse. When he found out that Francis was responsible for squandering these precious resources, he stormed down to San Damiano to seize Francis and bring him home.

When Francis heard that his father was approaching, he dropped his tools and ran for the hills. This was not one of Francis's finer moments. But after much prayer in the wilderness over several days, Francis plucked up his courage and returned to his project. He even went into Assisi and, dressed in rags, began begging for more building materials when supplies ran low.

When Peter Bernadone heard that his son was acting the part of a common beggar, he was both ashamed and enraged. He rushed to the square to apprehend him. This time Francis didn't run. His father dragged him home, beat him severely, and literally chained him in the basement until he came to his senses.

Jesus says, "Whoever does the will of God is my brother and sister and mother" (Mark 3:35). Even more harshly, he says in Matthew, "For I have come to set a man against his father, and a daughter against her mother, and a daughter-in-law against her mother-in-law; and one's foes will be members of one's own household. Whoever loves father or mother more than me is not worthy of me; and whoever loves son or daughter more than me is not worthy of me" (Matt. 10:35–37).

We tend to romanticize such sayings. We also tend to squeeze them into the mold of American individualism. So we are apt to resonate warmly with a character like Francis who, as the rugged spiritual individualist, pursues his personal sense of divine call despite the hostility of his family.

Francis' story is anything but a story of the rugged individualist, however, and a more thorough telling of this famous story can help snap us out of our cultural stupor. Francis indeed heard an individual and divine call on his life, but like most of us, it took him some time before he figured out what that exactly means. He began in a most literal way. But Francis is not remembered today as a great architect. It was only after fits and starts that he finally discovered that his mission was nothing less than the spiritual rebuilding of the universal church.

In the meantime, Francis got something else right—and wrong. He correctly perceived that many of the values by which he was nurtured (especially acquisitive materialism) were incompatible with this new calling. And he likely reacted as do many of us when we first realize how our upbringing has misled us—we become angry. We are shocked to discover that we have been raised in a way that the psalmist would call the way of destruction! I believe it was this combination of religious idealism and familial resentment that propelled Francis to steal from his family. But of course, in the fever of newfound religious enthusiasm, he didn't see it that way at all.

This, unfortunately, is the way it goes all too often when people experience the awe of a divine call. Combine that with the American myth that the true hero, the full adult, does not submit to any authority or community—especially not the family—but only to that inner sense of personal destiny. The result is the attitude that I *will* do it my way because to do anything less is to lead the quiet life of desperation and cowardice.

We've heard the stories of spiritual enthusiasm gone awry, and many of us, like Francis, in a fit of religious enthusiasm have "stolen" something—goods or time or affection—from our families. We have taken something without thought of giving in return. Stories of young believers leaving home prematurely, speaking judgmentally toward less-devout parents, denigrating the faith of their family, resenting their upbringing, mocking the dysfunctions of their family, or neglecting parents and siblings because they just don't understand spiritual matters: "They just don't get what I'm about." We stuff down the psychic pain this causes us because we believe that following God's will means denying one's family and doing what he wants us to do.

Francis was no hero at this point in his life. Though he had received a genuine call, so far he was nothing but a religious enthusiast who abused his family in the name of God. This business of first being a brother or sister of Christ has always been a lot harder than it looks.

When his father went away on a business trip, Francis managed to convince his mother to release him. He immediately made his way back to San Damiano to continue his mission.

When his father returned, he stormed off to find Francis. This time Francis would not be bullied. So his father returned to Assisi and filed suit against his son, but he was informed that since Francis was working for a priest, the city had no jurisdiction in this case. So his father appealed to the bishop of Assisi to intervene. Surely the bishop would not condone thievery.

He was right. In fact, Bishop Guido had a reputation for acquisitiveness himself. He owned substantial tracts of land around Assisi and knew the value of money. He immediately sent for Francis. Francis, a faithful son of the church, agreed to show up on the appointed day because he believed the bishop to be "the father and lord of souls."

Between the summons and the meeting, it appears that Francis had thought deeply about what he had done. He concluded that though his actions were wrong, his instincts were right. He pondered how he could clearly demonstrate that distinction at this meeting.

Francis, his father, and a handful of spectators gathered in the Piazza of Saint Mary Major, in front of the bishop's palace. After Peter Bernadone rehearsed his litany of complaints, Bishop Guido turned to Francis: "Your father is infuriated and extremely scandalized. If you wish to serve God, return the money you have, because God does not want you to spend money unjustly acquired for the work of the church."

"Lord," Francis replied, "I will gladly give back not only the money I acquired from his things." Francis stepped into a room in the bishop's palace, disrobed, folded his clothes in a neat pile, and then returned to the piazza. He stood before the assembly completely naked. He walked up to his father and presented him with the pile of clothes with a bag of money on top.

Francis turned to the onlookers: "Listen to me, all of you, and understand: Until now, I have called Peter Bernadone my father. But, because I have proposed to serve God, I return the money . . . and all the clothing that is his, wanting to say from now on, 'My father who is in heaven,' and not 'My father, Peter Bernadone.'"

Bernadone understood only too clearly what Francis was saying. He grabbed the clothes and money and stormed home. The bishop, moved with pity, wrapped Francis in his mantel until he could find some new clothes. Francis then made his way through the streets of Assisi, naked but for the bishop's mantel.

In his enthusiasm to do the will of God, Francis had acted clumsily. He needed to repent of that. What he couldn't repent of was the basic notion that it wasn't the will of his earthly father that was primary but the will of his Father in heaven. And most importantly, he recognized that his new call was not about him and him alone.

Francis' speech and act in the piazza was decidedly not about childhood rebellion or American individualism. It was, instead, a rejection of all that. His stealing of inventory and the family horse in the name of his call—that was rebellion; that was individualism. But in that piazza, Francis stood before the bishop's palace, having arrived there at the invitation of the church. And after being admonished by the bishop, his first act was to repent of his individualism, his idealism, his thievery.

To signal his new birth in the church, Francis stripped himself naked, entering into it as a babe comes into the world. He then entered his spiritual family, living among those who, as Jesus put it, seek to do the will of the Father in heaven. And when the bishop wrapped the vulnerable Francis in his mantel, it is not hard to see it as a symbol of Francis's now being clothed by, protected by, and identified with the church.

It is not a coincidence that before Jesus defined the family of God, Mark notes that he looked "at those who sat around him" (Mark 3:34). Jesus does not highlight a rugged individualist who is defying society or family in the name of God, but instead he points to a community gathered around him. It is only then that he says, "Here are my mother and my brothers! Whoever does the will of God is my brother and sister and mother" (vv. 34–35). The context is not the solitary religious hero but the people of God, gathered together around the person of Christ, seeking together the will of the Father.

It is mighty difficult, but we must resist the urge to see this passage as a confirmation or symbol of the unaccountable life, as encouragement for the solitary Christian to mine Scripture and pray alone in his closet to discern God's will for him and him alone. Instead, what we find here is another hard saying, another challenge to the soft faith of modernity that whispers the seductive lie, "The most important thing is the relationship between you and God; you don't need the church."

If our divine call entails the leaving of family—as some calls do—it is not a call to wander off alone into the world but to commit oneself to another family, to those Christ calls his brother and sister and mother—the church. This is a hard saying not just because we're individualists at heart but because the church is a corrupt and sin-laden institution. Many congregations are as dysfunctional as our families.

So why would we commit ourselves there? Because this is where Jesus says he is especially found—"For where two or three are gathered in my name, I am there among them" (Matt. 18:20). Among these two or three, or two or three thousand, Jesus will be found. They gather because they know the dangers of trusting one's solitary judgment in spiritual matters. They gather because they need the wisdom handed down in church tradition. They gather because they want their reading of Scripture informed by the larger reading of the community. They gather because they know it is in the community of those gathered around Jesus that they will hear, with ears to hear, more fully the will of God for their lives.

CHAPTER 8
Good Warnings

"Listen! A sower went out to sow. And as he sowed, some seed fell on the path, and the birds came and ate it up. Other seed fell on rocky ground, where it did not have much soil, and it sprang up quickly, since it had no depth of soil. And when the sun rose, it was scorched; and since it had no root, it withered away. Other seed fell among thorns, and the thorns grew up and choked it, and it yielded no grain. Other seed fell into good soil and brought forth grain, growing up and increasing and yielding thirty and sixty and a hundredfold." And he said, "Let anyone with ears to hear listen!"

Mark 4:3–9

At first I thought, *It's O.K. Nothing bad is going to happen.* A few seconds later the wave hit the road, and I thought, *Now I die.*

Tiina Seppanen, tsunami victim[1]

Those who have eyes to see can see a tsunami coming. If the trough of the wave hits the shore before the crest, the first thing you notice is the sea receding.

Tiina Seppanen was on vacation in December 2004 on Phuket Island in Thailand with her sister and mother when she noticed that the tide had gone way out. A vast, shiny expanse of sand had opened up, with fish flopping about. "People were saying it was something to do with the full moon," she said. Like children at a treasure hunt, they started shoving the fish into gunny sacks.

Then Seppanen saw the horizon rise and a wall of water approach, carrying with it small boats. "At first I thought, *It's O.K. Nothing bad is going to happen*," she said. "A few seconds later the wave hit the road, and I thought, *Now I die*."[2]

The tsunami moved faster than anyone's legs could carry them. One construction worker said that while a hysterical crowd in his village screamed as they ran toward higher ground, he and his wife and thirteen-month-old boy ran to a two-story house that lay between his village and the water. He climbed onto the roof with his family and survived.

But it wasn't just the first wave that was the danger. It was followed by the great sucking of the water back off the land—a rhythmic reversal that claimed thousands of lives. "I will never forget the screaming of those being washed out to sea," the construction worker said. Of the one hundred people in the village, he says only five survived.[3]

Besides the sea receding, there were larger warnings that also went unheeded. There was the massive earthquake at 7:58 a.m. off the Indonesia coast. A little more than an hour after the quake, Stuart Weinstein, the geophysicist on duty at the Pacific Tsunami Warning Center (PTWC) in Honolulu dispatched a bulletin to countries around the Pacific Rim, including Indonesia and Thailand, saying, "There is the possibility of a tsunami near the epicenter."

The official in charge of Indonesia's new tsunami warning system said that his office did indeed receive an email warning from the PTWC on the morning of December 26 but failed to see the message until the following day. Naturally, that was too late.

A description of one scene will suffice: In Bande Ache, the police and army closed off Lampase, a part of town between the seafront and the Ache River, to the public for almost a week while they cleared out thousands of bodies. Once security forces left, dazed fathers, mothers, sisters, and brothers wandered the rubble-strewn landscape searching for signs of missing loved ones. A *Time* magazine correspondent reported, "The neighborhood looks as though it has been backhanded by an enraged god. As far as the eye can see, only a few solitary buildings still stand. Littered everywhere are the achingly mundane contents of the houses: a sprinkling of playing cards, a bright yellow child's shoe, a shredded schoolbook."[4]

"Listen!" Jesus tells his disciples. "Warning! There is a possibility of a disaster. Let anyone who has ears to hear, listen!"

The Word of God is being scattered about:

> Those whose spirits are hardened—watch out! You will hardly have a moment to consider the truth before it seems like it is snatched from you.
>
> Those not deeply rooted in God—watch out! You are going to wither away as trouble or persecution strike.
>
> Those who pursue a comfortable and secure life—watch out! Your souls are being choked to death.

Indeed, there is good news for those who humbly receive the message of Jesus. Their lives will flourish. But most of the parable is a warning to the proud, the complacent, the worldly—those who think, *It's O.K. Nothing bad is going to happen.*

As Jesus's teaching unfolds, there are further warnings:

> Those who think they can hide their pride, shallowness, or worldliness—watch out. A day is coming when you will be exposed for who you are. "Let anyone with ears to hear listen!" (Mark 4:21–23).
>
> "Pay attention to what you hear." Whatever you give out in this life, that's exactly what you will get in return at the judgment (Mark 4:24).
>
> "Pay attention!" When all is said and done, if your life still amounts to nothing at the end, your worthless soul will be snatched from you (Mark 4:24–25).

And yet the people still rush out behind the suddenly receding tide to pick up the flopping fish.

The most troubling warning to modern readers, though, is the hinge between the telling and explaining of the parable of the soils. Jesus says something alarming to those who have sought him out:

> To you has been given the secret of the kingdom of God, but for those outside, everything comes in parables; in order that
>
> > "they may indeed look, but not perceive,
> > and may indeed listen, but not understand;
> > so that they may not turn again and be forgiven."
>
> Mark 4:11–12

We simply can't imagine Jesus wanting to do anything less than invite, as clearly and plainly as possible, *everyone* to participate in kingdom life. But here he seems to be saying that the secrets of that life are only given to some people.

Who? Those who take the trouble to go deeper, to ask more questions of Jesus. Those who ask, Jesus says elsewhere, will be given answers. Those who seek, will find. To those who knock, the door will be opened (Matt. 7:7–8).

But woe to those who don't seek—they will be inundated and then sucked away in the rhythm of judgment: We reject; God makes it harder for us to hear. We reject more; God makes it harder still. Like an even larger wave rolling in and a receding tide rhythmically pulling out with greater ferocity.

We are addicted to self like some are addicted to alcohol. One small drink leads to two, two leads to four, four can lead to drinking binges. And with each drink, it is more and more difficult to get control of oneself; the alcohol skews one's judgment and sabotages the will. The more one drinks, the harder it is to stop, the harder it is to hear people telling you that you must stop. Any alcoholic—anyone addicted to anything—will tell you that. How much more for those addicted to a self-centered existence.

To be fair to the whole witness of Scripture: even in the midst of a drinking binge, when the will seems to be utterly destitute of power—there can come the inner voice that says, "Enough! You are killing yourself. You don't have to do this anymore." Every addict knows such moments and knows that it is a moment of profound grace, moments when those who haven't had ears to hear suddenly hear.

In this haunting passage, Jesus warns people about the rhythm of judgment that begins with rejecting his Word. So once again, Jesus is being mean, stern—anything but the warm and fuzzy friend who blithely overlooks our shortcomings. He glares at our weaknesses, our addictions, our poor choices and says, "Watch out! Keep that up, and you are headed for disaster."

Jesus is not simply being mean; he's telling the truth. Some truths are stern. Some truths are sobering. When someone is in danger, telling the sobering truth can be the most loving thing one can do.

When a geophysicist warns people about a coming tsunami, it is a sign of compassion and concern. When a doctor warns a patient against smoking or eating fatty foods, he cares. And if doctors have to be a little stern, a little over-the-top to get their message across, we give them space to do that. We recognize that the consequences of not listening can be devastating.

Given our bad spiritual hearing, Jesus has to raise his voice, sometimes has to repeat himself, sometimes has to intimidate to get his point across. Thus in a passage that contains one hopeful bit of news—that those grounded in good soil will flourish—there are six warnings about the dire consequences of being hard-hearted. This uncomfortable ratio just shows how concerned, how compassionate, how loving the mean Jesus is.

Before Bill Curry was an ESPN analyst, he was a college football coach, and before that he was a lineman in the National Football League. Today he sports two Super Bowl rings. But in the spring of 1965, it was unclear whether he'd ever wear an NFL uniform. He had been drafted in the twentieth round by the Green Bay Packers of the Vince Lombardi era. He was convinced he would never make the team unless he gave himself an edge. So a few months before the tryouts, Curry began lifting weights—and taking steroids. They worked. He went from 220 to 240 pounds in just a few weeks.

When his father, a weightlifter himself, came to visit him, Curry excitedly told his dad about his accelerated improvement. "It's just incredible what these pills can do, Dad!"

His father asked, "Can I see the bottle?" He looked over the pills, walked to the bathroom, and began pouring them down the toilet. The younger Curry panicked, "What are you doing?"

His father then sat him down and warned him about steroids, how they would eventually destroy his body. Curry was shaken but convinced, and he never took steroids again. Today he simply says, "I'm so glad I had a father who loved me like that."[5]

There are thousands upon thousands of similar stories, where one person saved another from impending danger with a stern warning. And yet, so often when preachers warn people about the tsunami that will wreak havoc in their souls, they are considered negative, even judgmental. Or if a friend were to warn me about the spiritual dangers of, let's say, buying an expensive home that would put me in such debt it would sabotage my ability to give generously to the poor, I would probably think he was self-righteous and that this is really none of his business (even as I suspect he may be right).

Because we rightly fear being judgmental, self-righteous, or nosey, we hesitate to warn our friends and loved ones about the dangers Jesus so clearly talks about—even when we suspect that such a warning might do some lasting good. We cringe at the thought of speaking a sobering truth, even though it would indeed be an act of love.

If Jesus is to be trusted, our hesitancy is deadly for those who don't know Christ. It means, literally, nothing less than spiritual death. But it is equally deadly for those who claim to follow Christ—the church. Unless we learn once again to practice this ministry of warning, our churches will slowly slip into a lukewarm spirituality, one that makes Jesus so nauseous he'll want to spit us out (Rev. 3:16).

To be sure, nobody wants to be in a community of spiritual busybodies, where everyone is eyeing each other for vices and flaws, waiting for an opportunity to pounce. That's why, before we even consider the ministry of warning, we must first earn the right to be heard. I'm not likely to listen to someone I've just met. But I will pay close attention to the words of a friend who has prayed for and with me, who has both laughed and cried with me over the years.

This is one reason Jesus's warnings to us come across not as moralisms of a great religious teacher but as the stern counsel of an elder brother: he has identified with our weakness and died for our failures.

We are also wise to hold off our warnings until we've made it clear in word and deed that we, too, are in need of regular warnings. We have no business telling others about spiritual dangers if we are not vibrantly aware of the dangers we ourselves face—and open ourselves to the warnings of others.

In fact, our communities are best served when those who have failed the most in some area do most of the warning when it comes to that area. When I was a youth pastor, I tried to tell my youth group about the dangers of drinking, but it fell more or less on deaf ears—it was received as a wholesome lecture from one of the church's pastors. When one of the youth group sponsors, a man with a painful alcoholic past, said the same thing, the kids were mesmerized. They didn't miss a word.

The ministry of warning, then, is possible only when it is grounded in weakness and death. And this helps me discover a deeper reason I don't like to hear or give warnings. I squirm when I have to admit how weak I am and how I fight against dying to self. I prefer to give the impression that, except for a few peccadilloes here and there, I pretty much have my act together.

Because of this, we hesitate to dabble in the ministry of warning. We instinctively know our words will fall on deaf ears—just as the words of others fall on our deaf ears. We all feel the earthquake, yes, but it's O.K. Nothing bad is going to happen. Besides, we're admiring the vast expanse of shiny, wet sand that has suddenly appeared before us. And we're running about like children, with our bright yellow shoes and schoolbooks still in hand, combing the beach, laughing at the fish flopping in the sand.

CHAPTER 9
The Joy of Unfulfilled Desire

When he was alone, those who were around him along with the twelve asked him about the parables. And he said to them, "To you has been given the secret of the kingdom of God, but for those outside, everything comes in parables."

Mark 4:10–11

The true sight of God consists in this, that the one who looks up to God never ceases in that desire.

Gregory of Nyssa[1]

The golf swing is the most complex motion in all of sports, requiring an impossible combination of concentration and relaxation, rhythm and power, deliberation and letting go. There are a hundred points in the swing at which something can and usually does go wrong. Every club—and there are fourteen in one's bag—requires anywhere from a slightly altered to radically different swing. And we're not even on the golf course yet. Once there, all sorts of events unfold—hitting from behind a tree, gusting wind, downhill lies, and so on—that require one to alter one's shot even more. It is rare over the course of a lifetime to face two identical shots.

From the start, then, golf is an impossibility. There is no such thing as a perfect swing or a perfect game. But it is precisely this elusiveness that makes golfers so compulsive, so driven, so fascinated with the game. We leave the course frustrated because we fell so short of the perfection we imagined, and yet we return to the course as soon as possible because of that never-ending desire to reach perfection.

This paradox is true of any passion—gardening, music, writing, painting. The artist finds a measure of transcendence in painting a still life, but when done, she also sees how far short the image on the canvas falls. It is this frustration that prompts her to pick up the brush and oils and paint the same still life the next day and the next.

Anything we take passionately has this addictive quality. And so any human activity that engages us in this way can become like a spiritual discipline, a practice that can open us up to God.

As noted in the last chapter, the message of Jesus is veiled partly as an act of judgment. Jesus does not scatter the gospel indiscriminately before people who couldn't care less: "Do not give what is holy to dogs; and do not throw your pearls before swine, or they will trample them under foot and turn and maul you" (Matt. 7:6). Jesus, with deep sadness, respects people who are indifferent or who have hardened their hearts; he does not force himself on them. Yet the harder the heart, the harder it is to perceive, see, and be forgiven.

This veiling also reveals how God deals with everyone. Parables are given to both those whose hearts are soft and those whose hearts are hard. The Good News is veiled for all listeners. The gospel has an element of mystery, no matter who is at the receiving end. For those with hardened hearts, the mystery remains impenetrable. For those who seek out Jesus for an explanation, some of the mystery is removed—and at the same time, more mystery is encountered.

Those who have ears to hear have struggled for two thousand years not only with the precise meaning of verses 11 and 12 of the fourth chapter of Mark ("that they may indeed look, but not perceive") but especially the meaning of the parable's so-called explanation. Yes, Jesus's words explain a great deal, but we're still left with a great deal unexplained. The parable explains in part why some people never understand Jesus. But why exactly do some people have such hard hearts that they can't even begin to hear the gospel? Why do some people, when they have a taste of heaven, revert to chasing after the world? What exactly does all this suggest about the church's evangelistic task? Does it mean we should just give up on the hard-hearted and the worldly and only labor in more fruitful fields? For those who have ears to hear, there are still more questions.

The disciples come to Jesus to get answers, and they get some. But they also walk away with a lot more questions— questions that the church has had to struggle with since. This, in fact, is the pattern of salvation history. Many would truncate that history into a two-part drama: promise and fulfillment. The enslaved Israelites were promised liberation, and that promise was fulfilled. The nation of Israel was promised a Messiah, and the Messiah appeared. The church is promised the coming of the kingdom, and that kingdom will come.

But note how in each case the fulfillment is followed by another mystery, another enigma that causes the people of God to lean forward, to press for another unveiling. The newly liberated Israelites soon found that freedom created its own problems—thus the need for another fulfillment, the Messiah. And the coming of the Messiah left us with our current situation—the need for the complete coming of the kingdom of heaven.

And in the kingdom of heaven, do we imagine that all our questions will be answered and all our longings fulfilled? If we do, we are likely in for a big shock.

That our questions will remain unanswered and our longings unfulfilled is precisely the glorious nature of heaven. We are finite beings who are limited in knowledge, in space, and by time. In contrast to God, we will never know everything. In contrast to God, we can only be in one place at one time. In contrast to God, we had a beginning, thus our experience of time will always be limited by time.

But here is where we differ from the rest of the created order: God has placed eternity in our hearts (Eccles. 3:11). That is, we are aware that our knowledge is limited, and we can imagine an existence in which knowledge is unlimited. We are aware of the larger world and universe, and we know that we cannot inhabit it all at once, but we can imagine inhabiting it all at once. We can see how time constrains us, and we can imagine the concept of eternity. In short, since we are made in the image of an omniscient, omnipresent, eternal being, we have been given the gift of being able to imagine omniscience, omnipresence, and eternity. We have been given, in other words, the gift of the knowledge of God.

"The yearning to know What cannot be known, to comprehend the Incomprehensible, to touch and taste the Unapproachable, arises from the image of God in the nature of man," says spiritual writer A. W. Tozer. "Deep calleth unto deep, and though polluted and landlocked by the mighty disaster theologians call the Fall, the soul senses its origin and longs to return to its Source."[2]

This eternity in our hearts often frustrates us to such a degree that we take shortcuts to bridge the gap between our longing and its fulfillment. This is one way to define original sin. Adam and Eve felt they could not live with finite knowledge, and so they reached out for the knowledge of good and evil by eating of the very tree that God forbade. And with that one act, they became aware even more acutely of the gap between the eternity in their hearts and the finiteness of their nature. This in turn made them want all the more to close that gap prematurely.

Cain senses a gap between his longing for divine acceptance and his brother's apparent acceptance. Rather than work on his own soul, he thinks he'll simply eliminate the competition, leaving only him for God to love.

All sins are in one sense an attempt to fulfill a genuine, righteous longing, but in a way that is inappropriate. Augustine talks about this in his *Confessions*: "The soul commits fornication when she is turned from thee, and seeks apart from thee what she cannot find pure and untainted until she returns to thee." He then goes on to ask what the godly thing was he desired when he infamously stole a pear from a farmer's field. He finally concludes that he was seeking freedom "to rebel against thy law . . . so that, even as a captive, I might produce a sort of counterfeit liberty."[3]

As material beings, we want to enjoy the material blessings of this earth. We also long for sexual intimacy. We want to be respected and honored. Most of all, we want to know and be known by our Creator and to please him. But there are inappropriate ways to satisfy righteous longings, and since the time of Moses these inappropriate means have been given names: adultery, coveting, idolatry, and so forth.

But—and this is crucial— it isn't as if there is a righteous way to find complete fulfillment of any of our holy longings. To be sure, marriage is a wonderful place to attain a degree of sexual intimacy. Honesty and hard work are the divinely appointed means for earning and enjoying material blessings. Authentic worship of the invisible God is the path to a deeper relationship with him. Yes, God will give to those who seek, knock, and ask; he will fulfill our longings for wisdom and love—but only up to a point.

To be human is to be finite *and* to have eternity placed in our hearts, which means we know that we will forever exist as finite beings, with infinity—that is, perfect fulfillment of all our longings—just out of reach.

There is only one being for whom all longings have been completely fulfilled (so to speak), so much so that we say he is a being who has no needs. We are decidedly not that being, and we never will be. We will always, forever even in the kingdom, long for more.

Yet—and this is also crucial—this is not a frustrated longing, but an infatuated longing. When a young man and woman fall in love, they have found another person who suddenly fascinates them. This woman is the first person I think of when I wake up and the last person I think of before going to sleep. I relish every minute I spend with her. I ask her all sorts of questions about her life, her interests, her passions. The more I know, the more I realize I don't know, and my fascination becomes even more intense. When we fall out of love—out of this giddy, wonderful period—it's partly because we run out of energy to be continually fascinated. And we become bored and selfish and a host of other things. But the experience returns now and then throughout marriage, and it is this experience that reflects, I believe, the type of experience we'll have with God for eternity: an endless falling in love, an endless fascination, an endless pursuing of the mystery of God—and the fact that we are never fully satisfied is precisely one reason we'll find the kingdom of heaven such a joy.

"C. S. Lewis argued that love is most fully realized 'when what you most desire is out of reach,'" writes Belden Lane in his penetrating book, *The Solace of Fierce Landscapes*. "It is love's unattainability that draws us inexorably to it. Nothing is so unattainable as God, nothing more out of reach. Yet nothing evokes our love more strongly."[4]

Lane notes how this theme runs throughout Christian history. Anglican priest and metaphysical poet Thomas Traherne believed that human desire was the very image of God within us. Julian of Norwich says, "There is in God a quality of thirst and longing." As Lane sums up, "Human desire is simply a reflection of that original, irrepressible yearning in Christ."[5]

This is one reason the message of Jesus is elusive, why he speaks in parables that sometimes are nearly impenetrable and other times so layered with meaning that it could take an eternity to unravel their mysteries. It's the reason that God only slowly, over thousands of years, unveiled his plan for Israel and all the earth. It's the reason God refuses to show Moses anything but his backside. It's the reason Jesus toys with the Syrophoenician woman, Nicodemus, the woman at the well, and others. He rarely comes out and says plainly what it is he was trying to communicate. With the Syrophoenician woman he refers to "food" that is not worthy of "dogs" (Mark 7:25–30). To Nicodemus, he speaks about being born again (John 3:1–21). To the woman at the well, he speaks of water that will quench all thirst (John 4:7–15). Always elusive, always engaging, prompting the humble seeker to take the next step, to ask another question, to dig a little deeper.

The parable in Mark is one such example; it confused *everyone*. But it is only Jesus's most intimate disciples who take the trouble to find out more. They have fallen in love with the gospel, and they can't help but want to know more. They understand the rhythm of faith: promise, fulfillment, promise—for eternity.

"The true sight of God consists in this," writes the church father Gregory of Nyssa, "that the one who looks up to God never ceases in that desire."[6]

✠

This is precisely where large segments of modern Christianity, such as evangelicalism (a segment of the faith with which I happily identify), remain confused. We swallow mystery (that is, open-ended faith) with some difficulty.

The strength and glory of evangelical faith is this: we specialize in offering simple, clear, accessible explanations of Christian teachings. What could be more simple and direct than the Four Spiritual Laws? Evangelicalism is in part an ongoing reaction against a Christianity that becomes not just mysterious but convoluted and irrelevant. Evangelicalism is based on the love of neighbor, a yearning to communicate truth to the average person. And it has done this marvelously in its three-hundred-year history.

But at its worst, evangelicalism rationalizes the faith—crafts an explanation that "makes sense," that is too readily grasped with the mind. There is a temptation to systematize (thus all those dispensational charts) and to explain away all those difficult biblical passages (thus our enduring fascination with "The Bible Answer Man" and sermons that can take up to forty-five minutes of a sixty-minute worship service).

And thus the need to explain existence in Four Spiritual Laws. Laws—as if the mystery of God and his relationship with humankind can be grasped by a series of legal or scientific formulas. Where did we get the idea that this is the best way to describe a love affair?

Four laws? As if four, not five, not three, and not six hundred sum up the essence of the gospel. If this really can be done, one wonders why Jesus didn't do it in the first place. And one is mystified as to why he went about it so indirectly, in an aggravatingly roundabout way. Why didn't he just come to the point?

If the Four Spiritual Laws booklet is used to clarify some key points of the Christian message, and if that clarification allows a person for the first time to grasp some aspect of the Good News and to set his or her life on a new course—all well and good. Better than that—alleluia!

But if such formulas set one on a path of certainty, clarity, and fulfillment, then they will produce a faith that is a closed system, faith that brings only order to a confusing world, an order that becomes not a door into a greater mystery but a rigid wall outside of which one never ventures. Thus we get the worst aspects of evangelicalism: the rigidness, the legalism, the rationalism, the self-righteousness. This isn't all of evangelicalism to be sure, but enough of the movement shares these traits that they have become a not unfair way to characterize the movement.

Whenever we see this legalism, rationalism, and self-righteousness, we know that the faith has become a closed system—promise and fulfillment only. "Left to ourselves we tend immediately to reduce God to manageable terms," writes Tozer about mid–twentieth-century Christianity. But his words remain relevant today. "We want to get Him where we can use Him, or at least know where He is when we need Him. We want a God we can in some measure control. We need the feeling of security that comes from knowing what God is like."[7]

This is what Jesus saw in the Pharisees of his day. They had God in a box of rituals, laws, and explanations. There was no more to be unearthed, revealed, discovered. Spiritual fulfillment that led to no questions, no new mystery, and no new promise. Jesus rejects all this not just because of the hypocrisy or because of the lack of love but because "you lock people out of the kingdom of heaven. For you do not go in yourselves, and when others are going in, you stop them" (Matt. 23:13).

The kingdom of heaven is anything but a closed system: "The kingdom of God is as if someone would scatter seed on the ground," Jesus says, "and would sleep and rise night and day, and the seed would sprout and grow, he does not know how. The earth produces of itself, first the stalk, then the head, then the full grain in the head" (Mark 4:26–28). He continues, "It is like a mustard seed, which, when sown upon the ground, is the smallest of all the seeds on earth; yet when it is sown it grows up and becomes the greatest of all shrubs, and puts forth large branches, so that the birds of the air can make nests in its shade" (Mark 4:31–32).

So Jesus tweaks us once again with his meanness and wildness, just like the God he came to reveal: "Truly, you are a God who hides himself, O God of Israel, the Savior" (Isa. 45:15). Jesus urges us beyond our closed, comfortable systems. He teaches us slowly, elusively, in a way that requires patience and searching and more patience. The kingdom is a continual growing, expanding, and deepening of infatuation, he says. It is not a puzzle to be solved or an answer to be given or a system to be explained. The kingdom is that infuriating and delightful thing we call an obsession, like golf, or we call joy, like an eternal falling in love.

CHAPTER 10
Sobering Power

A great windstorm arose, and the waves beat into the boat, so that the boat was already being swamped. But he was in the stern, asleep on the cushion; and they woke him up and said to him, "Teacher, do you not care that we are perishing?" He woke up and rebuked the wind, and said to the sea, "Peace! Be still!" Then the wind ceased, and there was a dead calm. He said to them, "Why are you afraid? Have you still no faith?" And they were filled with great awe and said to one another, "Who then is this, that even the wind and the sea obey him?"

Mark 4:37–41

On the whole, I do not find Christians, outside of the catacombs, sufficiently sensible of conditions. Does anyone have the foggiest idea of what sort of power we so blithely invoke? Or, as I suspect, does no one believe a word of it?

Annie Dillard[1]

A group of Laotian refugees who had been attending the Sacramento church I pastored approached me after the service one Sunday and asked to become members. Our church had sponsored them, and they had been attending the church only a few months. They had only a rudimentary understanding of the Christian faith, so I suggested we study the Gospel of Mark together for a few weeks to make sure they knew what a commitment to Christ and his church entailed. They happily agreed.

Despite the Laotians' lack of Christian knowledge—or maybe because of it—the Bible studies were some of the most interesting I've ever led. After we read the passage in which Jesus calms the storm, I began as I usually did with more theologically sophisticated groups: I asked them about the storms in their lives. There was a puzzled look among my Laotian friends, so I elaborated: we all have storms—problems, worries, troubles, crises—and this story teaches that Jesus can give us peace in the midst of those storms. "So what are your storms?" I asked.

Again, more puzzled silence. Finally, one of the men hesitantly asked, "Do you mean that Jesus actually calmed the wind and sea in the middle of a storm?"

I thought he was finding the story incredulous, and I didn't want to get distracted with the problem of miracles. So I replied, "Yes, but we should not get hung up on the details of the miracle. We should remember that Jesus can calm the storms in our lives."

Another stretch of awkward silence ensued until another replied, "Well, if Jesus calmed the wind and the waves, he must be a very powerful man!" At this, they all nodded vigorously and chattered excitedly to one another in Lao. Except for me, the room was full of awe and wonder.

I suddenly realized that they grasped the story better than I did, and I finally acknowledged, "Yes, Jesus is a very powerful person. In fact, Christians believe he is the Creator of heaven and earth, and thus, of course, he has power over the wind and the waves."

This simplistic answer would not have gone over in some of the more sophisticated congregations of which I've been a part. As I noted, it didn't go over with me until I was confronted with my unbelief. The reasons for that are complex, but I think one is that the power of Christ frightens us—as well it should. And we'll do anything to avoid facing it as an ongoing reality, much to our loss.

We avoid the reality of Christ's power in a number of ways. For instance, we're tempted to spiritualize his power, to reduce the elemental potency and energy to a moment of personal religious inspiration. The stilling of the storm is about psychological storms in our lives. The healing of the lame is about solving emotional problems that cripple us. Jesus bringing sight to the blind is about God's ability to help us see our lives clearly. And so on and so forth. If we do that enough, we begin to think the Gospel stories are nothing but metaphors, and metaphors primarily about us.

We also try to rationalize Christ's power. The bald nature of miracles is an offense to modern sensibilities, so we do exegetical backflips to avoid offending those sensibilities. The so-called miracle of the loaves and the fishes was not about Jesus supernaturally multiplying food; instead, the miracle is that people were so moved by Jesus's message that they shared what they had with one another. The healing miracles are about the power of the mind over the body. As humorist Dave Barry says, I'm not making this up. Such vacuous sermons are preached in many mainline churches.

But a similar rationalization occurs in conservative churches. This happens especially on Easter Sunday when the preacher, knowing he'll face a sea of once-a-year, semireligious visitors, recognizes the anomaly the resurrection is. So he delivers a sermon that will explain, defend, and justify Jesus's rising from the dead with "evidences for the resurrection." The entire sermon strives to demonstrate that the resurrection makes sense, that it accords with reason, that it can slip easily into a compartment of our scientific minds. Let me be fair: I've preached this sermon!

It's not that the arguments for the resurrection are bogus. It's the inadequate assumption that arguments can "explain" or "make sense" of the resurrection. We imagine that once the case has been made, there's nothing more to be said. The resurrection is no longer an amazing, mysterious event, one pregnant with meaning and, yes, power. As Paul puts it, Jesus "was declared to be Son of God with power according to the spirit of holiness by resurrection from the dead" (Rom. 1:4).

Again, my Laotian friends understood this. When weeks later we read Mark's account of the resurrection, there was an awkward silence again. These people hadn't known how this Gospel ended, and they were flabbergasted. Finally, one younger woman shook her head and said, "I don't believe it. That's impossible. People don't rise from the dead!"

I said that I understood why it was hard to believe—it was indeed an astounding claim. I turned to a couple of the men and asked what their impressions were. They asked me if I believed it. I said I did. The elder of the group then said, "If the teacher believes it, we will too!"

There was a lot going on culturally in that statement, but it was clear to these novices that the resurrection was a huge stumbling block—as well it should be. They saw it for what it was—a scandalous act of divine power that demanded either rejection or submission.

A more subtle approach to the problem of divine power is to manipulate it. In this case, it looks like we very much believe in God's power when, paradoxically, it turns out we don't. I'm mostly thinking of the so-called prosperity gospel, in which people are taught formulas and attitudes that are said to more or less guarantee God's favor. Name it and claim it. Expect a blessing. Believe! And so on and so forth. If you have enough

faith, say the right prayer, and remain stubbornly persistent, God's power and blessing will become available to you.

Desperate people, of course, will use desperate means, and so I do not fault the common prosperity believer as much as their preachers and teachers, who should know better. Though critics of the movement stress the inevitable disappointment that such a message will produce, I think an equally large problem is, ironically, a lack of faith.

The god of the prosperity gospel is not the God of the prophets:

> Who has measured the waters in the hollow of his hand
>   and marked off the heavens with a span,
>   enclosed the dust of the earth in a measure,
>   and weighed the mountains in scales
>   and the hills in a balance?
> Who has directed the spirit of the LORD,
>   or as his counselor has instructed him?
>
> Isaiah 40:12–13

This God is utterly incapable of being manipulated by prayer formulas or positive thinking. He is more powerful and frightening than that.

Probably the most pervasive solution today is to completely subvert God's power, folding it into other gospel themes. Bookstore shelves are lined with upbeat, hopeful, cheery books about the love of God. One example will suffice. Note this Amazon.com description of the book, *Embracing the Love of God: The Path and Promise of the Christian Life*: "[The author] distills the basic principles of Christian love and provides a new model for relationship with God, self, and others that is based not on fear and judgment, but rather on acceptance and care. [His] moving insights illuminate the gentle nature

of God's love and teach readers how to continue on the path of love by embracing it day by day."[2]

"The gentle nature of God's love"? The author is surely not writing about the God of the Old and New Testaments, the God whose love is jealous and fierce, who destroys the Egyptian army on the way to delivering his beloved Israel, who chastises his beloved with exile, who, incarnate in Jesus Christ, vilifies the hypocrisy of the Pharisees, overturns the tables in the temple, calms the wind and the waves, and then scolds the disciples for their lack of faith. What god might this book be talking about?

That God's love includes "acceptance and care" there is no doubt. That his love can be reduced to this should be a scandal.

But we live in a sentimental age, and the temptation to sentimentalize God is ever with us. One nationally recognized church leader, for example, often waxes eloquent on God's softer attributes. In answering the question, "What is a compassionate heart?" he has repeatedly said this:

> St. Isaac of Syria asked this question many centuries ago, and here is his reply: "It is a heart that burns with love for the whole of creation—for humankind, for the birds, for the beasts, for the demons, for every creature. When a person with a heart such as this thinks of the creatures or looks at them, his eyes are filled with tears. An overwhelming compassion makes his heart grow small and weak, and he cannot endure to hear or see any suffering, even the smallest pain, inflicted upon any creature. Therefore he never ceases to pray, with tears even for the irrational animals, for the enemies of truth, and for those who do him evil, asking that they may be guarded and receive God's mercy."[3]

This preacher concludes, "Only the insistent and urgent compassion of Christ, enfolding the demons and reptiles that lurk in the secret places within us, can render us truly compassionate. And it is only the compassion of Christ worked in us

by the Spirit that can give us the expansiveness of heart which will allow us to extend our arms with the courageous and unwavering and all-embracing mercy of Christ himself."

One cannot help but be moved by this image of God enfolding in his arms all of creation. While I appreciate the preacher's good intentions, we need to recognize that this image is nearly the opposite of what we see in the Bible, especially the Gospels. To be sure, we see God as the faithful husband to Israel the harlot, and Jesus as the one who refuses to condemn the woman caught in adultery. At the same time—and this is the sort of thing many are tempted to ignore—Jesus does not embrace the demons but confronts them forcefully and casts them out. He does not ask that his enemies, the Pharisees, "be guarded and receive God's mercy," but he calls them hypocrites and warns them of the coming judgment if they do not repent.

Contra this preacher (who, it should be noted, took Isaac of Syria out of context), the God of the Bible is not an emotional wreck who bursts into tears when I accidentally step on my dog's foot. The true God is compassionate, but he is also a devouring fire (Deuteronomy 4), who told Israel, his beloved, "I will send my terror in front of you, and will throw into confusion all the people against whom you shall come" (Exod. 23:27).

He is the one who reveals his majesty to Isaiah, who saw God "sitting on a throne, high and lofty; and the hem of his robe filled the temple. Seraphs were in attendance above him; each had six wings: with two they covered their faces, and with two they covered their feet, and with two they flew. And one called to another and said: 'Holy, holy, holy is the LORD of hosts; the whole earth is full of his glory'" (Isa. 6:1–3).

God loves us so much he will not allow us to become comfortable with him. The god who makes us comfortable, the god toward whom we feel warm, the god who makes us feel good all the time. This is not the Creator of heaven and earth, the Lord and Savior—the only God who can save us, and save us in a way that is effective.

Eugene Peterson says that the Bible is interested not so much in whether we believe in God (it assumes most people do) but in our response to him:

> Will we let God be as he is, majestic and holy, vast and wondrous, or will we always be trying to whittle him down to the size of our small minds, insist on confining him within the boundaries we are comfortable with, refuse to think of him other than in images that are convenient to our lifestyle? But then we are not dealing with the God of creation and the Christ of the cross, but with a dime-store reproduction of something made in our image.[4]

In our fear—understandable fear—of the power and glory of God, we run and throw up our little temples and sacrifice to the manageable god of our imaginations. Jesus comes with might and wonder—in stilling real storms, in healing the truly blind, in raising the dead—to frighten us, and thus save us.

We tend to think there is nothing good that can come out of fear, and so verses like this one tend to mystify us: "Meanwhile the church throughout Judea, Galilee, and Samaria had peace and was built up. *Living in the fear of the Lord and in the comfort of the Holy Spirit*, it increased in numbers" (Acts 9:31, emphasis added). But time and again throughout Scripture, fear is connected with something wonderful. "The fear of the LORD is the beginning of wisdom" (Ps. 111:10). "The fear of the LORD is the fountain of life" (Prov. 14:27). The coming Messiah is one whose "delight shall be in the fear of the LORD" (Isa. 11:3).

We can get an inkling of this paradoxical truth when we think about something as simple as a campfire. "Be careful around fire," mothers say. They rightfully instill in their children a healthy sense of fear because fire can burn and maim and kill. But for all its danger, this fire is something that attracts us. We want to draw near to its light and warmth, especially on a cold and lonely night in the wilderness. And thus we delight in something about which we are rightly afraid.

The fearsomeness of the glory of God is delightful in another way—a way that makes the difference between life and death.

Early twentieth-century apologist G. K. Chesterton elucidates a similar idea when he talks about the "God of the Battles," the fierce God of the Old Testament, a deity whose power is made known in glorious victory over pagan idols. He notes the modern wish that Israel's God had been more of a friend, "stretching out his hands in love and reconciliation, embracing Baal and kissing the painted face of Astarte." It would have been easier for the Hebrews to "follow the enlightened course of Syncretism and the pooling of the pagan traditions." But, Chesterton notes, God was more loving than that:

> It is obvious indeed that His followers were always sliding down this easy slope; and it required the almost demoniac energy of certain inspired demagogues, who testified to the divine unity in words that are still like winds of inspiration and ruin, [to stop them]. . . . As it was, while the whole world melted into this mass of confused mythology, this Deity who is called tribal and narrow, precisely because He was what is called tribal and narrow, preserved the primary religion of all mankind. He was tribal enough to be universal. He was as narrow as the universe.[5]

To put it in terms of this chapter, God is loving enough to be fearsome. The God who is strong enough to defeat the enemies of Israel, mighty enough to wrestle the Evil One to the mat and destroy his power, the one powerful enough to defeat death and raise us to new life—this God has a potency that, when revealed to us, will make us tremble because of its ferocity. How could it do anything else?

In the end, there is no dichotomy between the fear of the Lord and the comfort of the Lord. It is his might and glory that accomplishes both, and not one without the other. In Isaiah 40 we find a nearly perfect coupling of these ideas. The God who inspires fear and awe—

> Have you not known? Have you not heard?
> The LORD is the everlasting God,
>   the Creator of the ends of the earth.
> He does not faint or grow weary;
>   his understanding is unsearchable. . . .

is the same God who brings us comfort and strength—

> He gives power to the faint,
>   and strengthens the powerless.
> Even youths will faint and be weary,
>   and the young will fall exhausted;
> but those who wait for the LORD shall renew their strength,
>   they shall mount up with wings like eagles,
>   they shall run and not be weary,
>   they shall walk and not faint.

> Isaiah 40:28–31

This is the God who came to us in Jesus Christ, the mean and wild one who stormed through Galilee, stilling violent rains, healing the disfigured, and raising to life those whose bodies had gone stone cold dead. And when he did such things, he filled people with fear and awe—and an unwavering confidence in his power to deliver us from evil.

CHAPTER 11
Mercifully Irrelevant

Then he began to teach them that the Son of Man must undergo great suffering, and be rejected by the elders, the chief priests, and the scribes, and be killed, and after three days rise again. He said all this quite openly. And Peter took him aside and began to rebuke him. But turning and looking at his disciples, he rebuked Peter and said, "Get behind me, Satan! For you are setting your mind not on divine things but on human things."

Mark 8:31–33

Woe to the person who smoothly, flirtatiously, commandingly, convincingly preaches some soft, sweet something which is supposed to be Christianity!

Søren Kierkegaard[1]

On a recent trip I had a chance to attend one of the most successful churches in America. It packs in over twenty thousand people in its weekend services. Its pastor is the author of bestselling books and is a world figure. The church is inspiring, effective, and relevant.

Fortunately, it became impossible to attend there, and instead I was blessed to end up at an irrelevant church. Our family arrived promptly at 10:00 a.m., and we were greeted by a woman who had just finished pulling a few weeds in front of the church sign. She welcomed us warmly and escorted us into the nearly empty sanctuary. As we sat and waited for the service to begin, we were greeted by two other people as well as the pastor. Finally, at about ten minutes after the hour, a handful of people straggled in and worship began.

We were led in music by the weed-puller, who now had a guitar strapped on. She was accompanied by two singers and an overweight man on percussion. They were earnest musicians who, frankly, were sometimes flat or a little stiff, as if they were still trying to learn the music. The service, which included maybe forty-five people, bumbled along— that is, by contemporary, professional, "seeker-sensitive" standards. The dress of the congregants suggested that some were people of substance and others were on welfare. Some blacks, mostly whites. In front of me sat a woman wearing way too much makeup (at least according to my suburb's standards), poofy hair, and an all-black outfit. Next to her was her mousy-looking husband.

Communion was offered before the sermon, and it was introduced without the words of institution—a bit of a scandal to my Anglican sensibilities. The pastor took prayer requests, and petitions were made for illnesses, depression, and safe travel for my family.

It was during the announcements that I began to suspect I was in the midst of the people of God. In seeking more donations for the food closet, the pastor noted a new milestone for the church: they had served 22,000 people with groceries in ten years. Everyone applauded, and then they settled in to hear a clear and truthful sermon about God's love for us despite our sin.

Afterward my family was warmly greeted by another five or six people, one of whom invited us to lunch. It was evident that they really didn't care that we were not coming back. They just wanted to make sure we felt welcomed.

Nothing slick. Nothing professional. No studied attempts to be authentic or relevant or cool. Just a small bunch of sinners, of all classes and races, looking to God for guidance and reaching out to the community in love.

This little church will never make the list of the top ten churches in America. It will never be featured in *Time* or *Newsweek* or even *Christianity Today*. Its musicians will not go on to record a CD; its pastor will not be invited to national preaching conferences. The church will not likely grow into the thousands.

I'm sure that had I attended the megachurch, I would have been inspired by the music, moved by the message, impressed with the professionalism and efficiency of the service, and comfortable sitting next to people who dressed like me, an upper-middle-class suburbanite. But it was a more godly experience to go to that little fellowship because I believe that, for all the good the megachurch does, this little fellowship manifested the presence of Jesus in a way that is unique and absolutely necessary in our age.

From the beginning, Christians have been tempted to confuse success with faith. Peter was the first one to succumb to the confusion.

When Jesus reveals to the disciples that he will be killed, Peter is scandalized. He has imagined, I suppose (for the text doesn't really say), that Jesus was moving from success to success. He had started with a small band of twelve, and lately he has had up to five thousand attending his little talks. He has challenged the authorities of the day, but given his popularity, they have been unable to lay a hand on him. Peter imagines, as do many in his day, that when Jesus speaks about the coming kingdom, he is talking politics—Peter and the disciples will someday be cabinet members of his coming administration. Power. Glory. Success.

Jesus knows very well that this pandering after success and respectability is a temptation for his disciples, and he has spent his whole ministry trying to disabuse them of it. He told those whom he has healed not to tell anyone—an inept marketing decision if there ever was one. He told bickering disciples that they should worry less about who will have authority in the coming kingdom and more about serving one another.

Then Jesus tells them that the success of his ministry will culminate in his death. Peter will hear no such thing and starts rebuking Jesus, presumably for such negativity.

Jesus in turn rebukes Peter—this is a biblical euphemism for "an argument broke out." As is fitting, Jesus has the last word: he calls Peter a student of Satan and tells him to stop measuring success by human standards.

Since Peter is understandably confused—nearly everyone thought of the kingdom in political terms—Jesus seems a bit mean to chastise Peter so strongly: satanic, disciple of the devil, evil. Not the most diplomatic approach in any circumstance. But apparently Jesus thinks Peter's confusion is not just a misunderstanding but a betrayal.

Today we know all too well that the kingdom of God is not a political entity (though many Christians on both the left and right are sorely tempted to think otherwise). But we still, like Peter, pander after a gospel of glory and power. We make much ado about our Christian superstars—best-selling authors, platinum-selling musicians, and powerful preachers who draw in listeners by the tens of thousands. We not only admire but we lift up and reward such success. We too easily think that growing numbers is an infallible sign of faithfulness. We confuse righteousness with arithmetic.

Conservative churches, for example, often compare themselves with liberal churches and like to point out how liberal churches are shrinking and conservative churches are growing. The usually unspoken assumption is that such growth signals God's blessing.

Though assumed to be a sign of God's blessing, church growth has actually become a mere science. Today when people want to start a church, the first thing they do is study the people they are trying to reach, and they then craft worship and ministry to meet the needs of that target audience. That is, church founders do their best to appear acceptable and relevant to their target audience.

To minister to college-educated, upwardly mobile twenty- and thirty-somethings—the target of a lot of new ministries these days (whatever happened to preaching to the poor and the prisoners?)—you wear Abercrombie clothes, forbid hymns and organ music, and preach (no, make that "share") without a pulpit, wearing an open knit shirt, jeans, and flip-flops. And it works, because lots of churches that do this sort of thing are bursting at the seams with twenty- and thirty-somethings.

It's gotten to the point that there is no shame left. *Christianity Today* columnist Andy Crouch once attended what he called a "distressed-jeans, multiple-piercings forum." He was talking with a twenty-five-year-old pastor with styled hair who told him bluntly, "Yeah, we're starting a church for cool people."

When Crouch asked for clarification, the pastor replied, "Yeah, you know, people like us."

Crouch was not sure he would fit in, but by the end of the weekend, this pastor told him, "You know, dude, you may not have cool hair, but you have some serious clue."[2]

Donald Miller, a thirty-something himself, talks about a similar experience in *Blue Like Jazz*. He has a pastor friend who started a new church. It was going to be different from the old church, Miller was assured: it will be relevant to the culture and the human struggle.

Miller wisely notes, "If the supposed new church believes in trendy music and cool Web pages, then it is not relevant to culture either. It is just another tool of Satan to get people to be passionate about nothing."[3]

I think it is not an accident that Miller, like Jesus, uses the *S* word to talk about what is threatened here. To pander after relevance, success, effectiveness, and glory—this is not just a slight misunderstanding of the gospel but its very betrayal. It is not error. It is, according to Jesus, satanic.

Philosopher Søren Kierkegaard makes a similar point when he imitates the passage in Matthew's Gospel (chapter 23) in which Jesus speaks his harshest judgment on the religion of his day:

> Woe to the person who smoothly, flirtatiously, commandingly, convincingly preaches some soft, sweet something which is supposed to be Christianity! Woe to the person who makes miracles reasonable. Woe to the person who betrays and breaks the mystery of faith, distorts it into public wisdom, because he takes away the possibility of offense! . . . Oh the time wasted in this enormous work of making Christianity so reasonable, and in trying to make it so relevant![4]

Fortunately, embedded in this argument between Peter and Jesus is just the mercy we need. Jesus's rebuke to Peter—and the implied rebuke to us today—turns out to be the most gracious thing he could have done. Sometimes Jesus's rebuke comes in the form of words, but most of the time it comes in the warp and woof of Christian living.

The first church I served after seminary offered a traditional Presbyterian worship service. Old hymns, written prayers, formal and, to me, stiff throughout. I remember looking out over the congregation during one interminable communion service and feeling sorry for the congregation because they had to endure this empty ritualism. During the service, I read the prayers the senior pastor had asked me to read, but in between, I imagined myself in my own church and how I would make worship really relevant to the culture!

After the service, one elderly woman smiling broadly approached me and pumped my hand in gratitude. "Thank you so much for helping with the service," she bubbled forth. "It was one of the most meaningful communions I have experienced in years."

I was shocked, and it took a few weeks for this to sink in. But sink in it did as I informally conducted a survey of parishioners. Lo and behold, most of them found our services moving and meaningful. I felt the rebuke of Jesus: "What is 'relevant,' 'meaningful,' and 'powerful,' is more mysterious than you imagine."

Like many young pastors, I was afflicted with an ungodly idealism. I believed that a church made in my image—an image I was convinced was formed only by the Bible, deep theology, and my own uncommon spirituality—was the church of God's dreams. Theologian Dietrich Bonhoeffer warned about such idealism in his now classic *Life Together*: "He who loves his dream of community more than the Christian community itself becomes a destroyer of the latter, even though his personal intentions may be ever so honest and earnest and sacrificial."[5]

The relevant community of faith we imagine is usually a combination of biblical, cultural, and personal expectations, some of them so deeply embedded in our psyches that we just assume they are truly righteous. Because they are dreams, they usually have little to do with the reality called *the church*. When we try to fashion the church in our image, the result so often is anger, division, and hostility. Pastors (and I was no exception) chalk this up to the price of being prophetic lead-

127

ers. But often it's merely a pandering after ecclesial success of our own image. And we sometimes end up destroying the very community we had come to save.

The reality of that community—the Christians really there, acting like they usually do—is a shocking disappointment to the dreamer. The church is indeed often boring and irrelevant. Its leaders bicker, its members gossip, and its building can be an embarrassment to modern sensibilities (aesthetic and environmental). The old charge remains true: the church is full of hypocrites. The typical church in history—the typical church today—has little to commend itself in the way of glory, power, and success.

Yet it is this institution—not our dream institution—with which Christ chooses to be identified. He has put his very name on it, calling it his body. He endorses it and tells us to draw people into this institution if they are to come to know him genuinely.

Along the way, Jesus works ever so hard to snap us out of our illusions. Bonhoeffer puts it this way:

> By sheer grace, God will not permit us to live even for a brief period in a dream world. He does not abandon us to those rapturous experiences and lofty moods that come over us like a dream. God is not a God of the emotions but the God of truth. Only that fellowship which faces such disillusionment, with all its unhappy and ugly aspects, begins to be what it should be in God's sight, begins to grasp in faith the promise that is given to it.[6]

What the church should be in God's sight is not glorious, powerful, or successful by our standards, but faithful. This means the church, and every member in it, must die to dreams of relevance and success. We have to let all that be crucified. It also means letting the church be the church, the flawed institution that God has used time and again to further his kingdom in the world.

We rightfully glory in the Reformation, a time when theologians such as Martin Luther, John Calvin, and Thomas Cranmer led the church through a desperately needed reform. But we should remember that those theologians were nurtured in the moribund church they eventually reformed. The Great Awakening was a wonderful time of church renewal in America and Britain. But the preachers who brought revival—George Whitefield, John and Charles Wesley, and others—were nurtured and raised in "dead" churches. Somewhere in that irrelevant environment, God worked in and through the church to renew them, and through them, the entire church.

We are not wise to merely disparage successful megachurches, which often are catalysts for significant change. What we should repudiate in the strongest terms—as Jesus did—is the notion that these churches represent the true church, the glorious church, the epitome of success.

To be sure, the church is in constant need of reform—some eras more than others—and so we need our reformers and, yes, visionaries, many of whom these days find their way into "successful" churches. But in every era God raises up reformers within the irrelevant, unsuccessful churches that need reform. *Relevance* and *power* and *success* are finally a mystery, not so much something that can be manipulated by church growth science as something to pray for in humility and faith.

Jesus loves us so deeply that he sometimes slaps our vague idealism in the face with a healthy dose of reality. This shocks us, and we find ourselves speechless and blushing with either anger or shame. Not only do we not have the cool church we had hoped for, we don't have an understanding Lord to comfort us through our faith crisis! Instead Jesus just rebukes us harshly with this reality and tells us to stop betraying his cause by worshipping false gods.

Like Peter, we have to die to our notions of relevance and success and let God—through a crucified Savior, through an amateurish church, through a stiff communion service—raise up his people when he will and how he will, with a power and glory we can hardly imagine.

CHAPTER 12
Really High-Demand Religion

If any want to become my followers, let them deny themselves and take up their cross and follow me. For those who want to save their life will lose it, and those who lose their life for my sake, and for the sake of the gospel, will save it.

Mark 8:34–35

Happy are they who have reached the end of the road we seek to tread, who are astonished to discover the by no means self-evident truth that grace is costly just because it is the grace of God in Jesus Christ.

Dietrich Bonhoeffer[1]

Since Dean Kelly's 1972 classic, *Why Conservative Churches Are Growing*,[2] a lot has been written about high-demand churches—in particular, Christian churches that expect their members to adhere to orthodox doctrine and live by traditional Christian morality. These churches are contrasted with low-demand churches, usually mainline churches (such as Presbyterian, Methodist, Congregational, and Episcopal). Sociologists of religion note that high-demand churches—usually evangelical and charismatic churches—are attracting more and more people, and that low-demand churches are losing members.

Take, for example, the analysis of Laurence R. Iannaccone of Santa Clara University in his influential essay, "Why Strict Churches Are Strong." Iannaccone defines strictness as "complete loyalty, unwavering belief, and rigid adherence to a distinctive lifestyle."[3] Strict churches, he shows, are more likely to grow and remain strong than churches that have lower expectations in terms of both belief and behavior.

Some would question whether megachurches—the most visible symbol of growing conservative churches—are growing because of their high demands. The rap on them is that they grow precisely because they make no demands. Most of them, to be sure, make no demands on people who attend. But the closer you get to membership, and then the more responsibility you take on in such a church, the higher the demands. The doctrinal assumptions (the Trinity, divinity of Christ, virgin birth, the authority of Scripture, and so forth) and ethical standards (honesty, sexual purity, sacrificial love, and so forth) that undergird the preaching and teaching are nothing to scoff at. In an increasingly pluralistic and hedonistic culture, these are indeed *demands.*

So why do people like such churches? Iannaccone argues doctrinal and behavioral strictness "increases commitment, raises levels of participation, and enables a group to offer more benefits to current and potential members." Consequently, he says these groups "enjoy a competitive advantage over their opposites (who suffer from less commitment, lower participation, and fewer perceived benefits)." "Strict churches," he concludes, "proclaim an exclusive truth—a closed, comprehensive and eternal doctrine. They demand adherence to a distinctive faith, morality, and lifestyle. They condemn deviants, shun dissenters, and repudiate the outside world."[4]

Baylor University sociologist Rodney Stark argues the same point in a number of books, especially those in which he analyzes historical patterns of church growth.[5] "People value religion on the basis of cost," he told one interviewer, "and they don't value the cheapest ones the most. Religions that ask nothing get nothing. You've got a choice: you can be a church or a country club. If you're going to be a church, you'd better offer religion on Sunday. If you're not, you'd better build a golf course, because you're not going to get away with being a country club with no golf course."[6]

We who identify with evangelical churches might conclude, rather proudly, that we're in the perfect faith then. For our Lord is not the least bit interested in founding a country-club religion:

> If any want to become my followers, let them deny themselves and take up their cross and follow me. For those who want to save their life will lose it, and those who lose their life for my sake, and for the sake of the gospel, will save it.
>
> Mark 8:34–35

> If your hand causes you to stumble, cut it off; it is better for you to enter life maimed than to have two hands and to go to hell, to the unquenchable fire.
>
> Mark 9:43

> Children, how hard it is to enter the kingdom of God! It is easier for a camel to go through the eye of a needle than for someone who is rich to enter the kingdom of God.
>
> Mark 10:24–25

133

High-demand indeed. So there we have it. A high-demand Lord, who creates high-demand churches, to which people flock more than ever. Demanding *and* popular—a religion with the best of both worlds.

We have to be honest with ourselves. Conservative, traditional, growing churches are demanding only up to a point. It's not hard to find Christian churches or communities that are significantly more demanding than these popular conservative churches.

Take monasteries or convents, for example, with their very high demands of poverty, chastity, and obedience. These theologically conservative and morally strict communities are not winning converts by the tens of thousands. As many people attend weekly services at one charismatic church in Houston (about 30,000) as there are Franciscan friars worldwide.[7]

Or take the movement called "the new monasticism." In the last decade or so some two dozen communities have been founded in inner cities across America. Young men and women, some single, some married, have agreed to live in the same part of the city—usually one of the poorest sections—and practice the traditional spiritual disciplines together (prayer, fasting, Bible study, and so forth) while ministering to prostitutes, drug addicts, single mothers, the homeless. To honor and serve Jesus, these young people are forsaking lucrative careers and safe lifestyles.[8] High-demand indeed, but you only see dozens following this path, not thousands.

So it seems we want some theological and moral demands made on us, but just not too many. Give us a *somewhat challenging* faith and we do just fine.

Then along comes Jesus, telling us to cut off a hand or foot or cut out an eye if it gets in the way of serving him. He instructs us to abandon wives, sisters, brothers, and friends and put our lives on the line. I don't know about you, but I'd much rather tithe, pray daily, serve on a couple of church committees, lead a men's Bible study, serve on the church board, and attend weekly worship. As exhausting as it is to be a good churchman, it's infinitely easier than the demands Jesus would make on my life.

Though I might admire monks, nuns, and the new monastics, even their high demands pale in comparison to what Jesus asks. Poverty, chastity, obedience—child's play when stacked up against self-mutilation and self-sacrifice!

Scholars are quick to point out that Jesus is, of course, speaking in hyperboles. He is exaggerating to make a point. There is a certain amount of wisdom in that interpretation. The early church father, Origen, castrated himself so that one particular part of his body would not cause him to fall. Nobody then or since has taught that this is the sort of thing Jesus—the Creator of bodily life and therefore the one who blesses bodily life—would approve of in the end.

Self-mutilation, hyperbole. Self-sacrifice? I think not. We have many biblical examples of people forsaking family (from Abraham to Peter) or giving up their lives (deacon Stephen being the first) for the sake of Jesus. Even when biblical heroes don't literally move away from their families or give up their lives, there is this sense that family is to come second and that one's entire life should be focused first and foremost on Christ.

The point is simply this: if we've given ourselves to a contemporary, high-demand expression of faith, we should recognize that it doesn't even approach the demands Jesus makes on us. Even monastics, old and new, know that their sacrifices are ridiculously meager. And when this reality hits us from time to time—as well it should, if we're at all honest with ourselves—the only reasonable reaction is fear and trembling. What else would a sane person do after realizing that Jesus wants nothing less than all of us—every molecule, every breath, every ounce of energy, every interest, every passion, every thought, every action, every love? It certainly scares the bejeebers out of me.

"Then who can be saved?"

That's the disciples' reaction when Jesus tells them how hard it is for the wealthy to be saved (Mark 10:25–26). They are "exceedingly astonished" (ESV) at his comparison—it's easier for a camel to go through the eye of a needle than it is for a rich man to enter the kingdom of heaven—because they saw that it applies to everyone. They ask not, "Then what *rich man* can be saved?" but "Can *anyone* be saved?" It's the same reaction we have after honestly staring at the gap between our lives and Jesus's demands.

Jesus, of course, reminds us that our despair is not the last word: "With man it is impossible, but not with God. For all things are possible with God" (Mark 10:27 ESV). The same Jesus who makes unreasonable and impossible demands on us is able to sympathize with our weakness and patiently endure our selfishness. If his demands are high and lifted up, his mercy is as wide as the East is from the West.

We look to the top of the spiritual Everest that Jesus expects us to climb, and our hearts sink. We didn't bring the right boots. We don't have enough water, nor a single oxygen tank, nor ice picks, nor climbing rope. We have no idea how to scale steep, icy slopes. And we're so out of shape, we can barely walk back and forth from the campfire to our tent.

But Jesus, our gentle, patient Sherpa, doesn't expect us to get to the top of the mountain in the next couple of hours. He will never let us forget what the impossible goal is, but he is merciful. He will train us up in the way that we should go. He will supply all our needs. He will patiently endure those times when we go two steps forward and three steps back.

Along the way there will be times when we're pretty proud of the progress we've made, and we'll be tempted to sit by the trail and bask in our accomplishments, noting how much further we've gotten than those mainline hikers way back there. But then we'll look ahead and see how very far the peak is, shrouded in mysterious clouds, intimidating, frightening, yet pulling us upward. There will be times we'll have to walk along dangerous precipices, and we'll wonder, in fear, what we've gotten ourselves into. And some days, our legs will shake and our lungs will sting, and we won't be able to imagine going on any further.

But we'll know that no matter how demanding the journey, no matter how weak and unprepared we feel, no matter how frightened we are at times, there is no turning back from the upward call. It is hard. But it is our destiny. And we gladly (at least most days) accept the fearsome demands it makes on us.

This mountain-climbing image, however, gets at only part of what's going on. For Jesus's demands are made not simply to get us to a holy destination or to make us better people. In the end, all these high demands are about love.

At various times in our marriage, my wife and I have had to do the difficult, demanding, and scary work of deepening our intimacy. There are times when we realized we'd reached a plateau, and we could either coast to retirement and death at that level or we could decide to go deeper. So far, we've always decided to go deeper.

The very thought of doing that frightens both of us because to deepen our love means we have to make some frightening demands on ourselves and on one another. We have to tell each other even more things we would just as soon keep confidential. We've had to push each other to talk when all either of us wanted to do was run from the conversation. We've had to hear ourselves tell each other painful, searing truths about one another. These are high-demand moments in a marriage, and they are miserable moments, frightening moments. There are times when the very marriage seems to hang in the balance if we don't get through this one conversation.

We admit we don't do this intimacy thing very well. We hesitate; we balk; we do it in fits and starts. But when we're willing to make these extraordinary demands on ourselves, we enter into a deeper knowledge of one another, a deeper love for one another.

If couples love each other enough to make such demands on one another, is it hard to imagine that Jesus makes demands on us precisely because he loves us and because he wants us to know him more intimately and love him more deeply?

CHAPTER 13
Gracious Impatience

You faithless generation, how much longer must I be among you? How much longer must I put up with you?

Mark 9:19

It is the essence of the sin of the Garden to re-imagine God into the mythical tolerant god.

Dean Waldt[1]

At the end of each school year of high school, my children's attentiveness to household chores would inevitably slip. Finals, end-of-the-year parties, concerts, and award ceremonies left little time for vacuuming, emptying the garbage, and doing the dishes, let alone picking up after themselves. But I understood their plight, so I often found myself doing their chores during these times.

Though I was being patient, my children sometimes mistook my actions for indifference. So, when finals ended and summer began, they would sometimes not quite get back into the chores routine. I'd remind them that it was their turn to do the dishes, and they'd say, "Sure, Dad, I'll get to them later." But I'd waken the next morning to find the kitchen sink overflowing with crusted plates.

It wasn't until I confronted them sternly, with an impatient tone and a hard stare, that they realized that I hadn't been indifferent but merely patient. To be sure, I wanted the dishes done, but I also didn't want them to grow up to be people who didn't keep their word. So, ironically, it was my impatience that communicated that I really loved them.

The psalmist reminds us, "The LORD is merciful and gracious, slow to anger and abounding in steadfast love" (Ps. 103:8). But when the Lord was incarnate among us, he regularly showed flashes of anger and impatience.

When the Pharisees approach him and begin arguing with him, Mark tells us that Jesus "sighed deeply in his spirit and said, 'Why does this generation ask for a sign? Truly I tell you, no sign will be given to this generation'" (Mark 8:12). We certainly understand Jesus's impatience. Who is expected to be forbearing with self-righteous hypocrites?

One scholar considers that passage "the nadir of dismay" in Mark's Gospel.[2] Not quite. Jesus seems to be even more disconcerted by his disciples, his intimate friends. One day as Jesus and the disciples make their way across Lake Galilee, the disciples begin mumbling to one another that someone had forgotten to bring bread—and this just after Jesus had fed the four thousand. Overhearing their talk, Jesus tells them enigmatically that they should beware of the yeast of the Pharisees. The disciples are dumbfounded by this comment, as we might expect. It seems to have come out of the blue. But when Jesus notices their perplexity, he just scolds them: "Do you still not perceive or understand? Are your hearts hardened?

Do you have eyes, and fail to see? Do you have ears, and fail to hear?" (Mark 8:17).

This impatience is less understandable because it seems unfair to expect these men to pick up Jesus's odd metaphorical cues. But perhaps Mark is suggesting that having spent so much personal time with Jesus they should have had a little more faith by now. So maybe Jesus's impatience is understandable here after all.

Then again, Jesus seems to be an equal opportunity scolder. Just a bit later we find him laying into common people. After the father of an epileptic boy anxiously explains that the disciples were unable to heal his son, Jesus blurts out, "You faithless generation, how much longer must I be among you? How much longer must I put up with you?" (Mark 9:19).

Not exactly the Jesus meek and mild we've gotten used to. Love is patient, says Paul. But what sometimes looks like patience is not necessarily love, says Jesus.

The civil rights movement is one of the most dramatic illustrations of the point. When Martin Luther King Jr. led marches and boycotts in Birmingham, Alabama, in 1963, the local white ministerial association chided him for his impatience with the judicial process. Wait, they said, and things will slowly get better.

King would have none of it. He asked them how he and his friends could wait when they had seen vicious mobs lynch their mothers and fathers, had watched hate-filled policemen curse, kick, and kill their black brothers and sisters, had witnessed the vast majority of 20 million blacks "smothering in an airtight cage of poverty in the midst of an affluent society." He wondered why he should be patient when time and again he found himself tongue-tied as he tried to explain to his six-year-old daughter why she couldn't go to the public amusement park she'd seen advertised on television, seeing tears well up in her eyes when he had to tell her that Funtown is closed to black children, and then watching "ominous clouds of inferiority beginning to form in her little mental sky, and see her beginning to distort her personality by developing an unconscious bitterness toward white people."[3]

King asked the ministerial association how he could wait any longer when his first name had become "nigger," his middle name "boy," and his wife and mother were never given the respected title of "Mrs." How could he continue to wait, to be patient, he asked, "When you are harried by day and haunted by night by the fact that you are a Negro, living constantly at tiptoe stance, never quite knowing what to expect next, and are plagued with inner fears and outer resentments; when you [are] forever fighting a degenerating sense of 'nobodiness.' . . . There comes a time when the cup of endurance runs over," he told them, "and men are no longer willing to be plunged into the abyss of despair."

Because Martin Luther King Jr. cared for his fellow blacks, because he was concerned about whites (knowing that their racism was destroying their souls), because he cherished America and its ideals of freedom, he could be patient no longer. He loved so much, he had become impatient and intolerant of racism and injustice.

We often confuse patience and tolerance. But between them lies an eternity of difference.

To tolerate others you don't have to agree with them; you don't have to like them. You simply allow them to exist unmolested, to peacefully coexist with you. You respect their personal choices and refrain from imposing your personal choices on them. If you seek to convince others that their choices are morally wrong, harmful, or even evil, and that your choice is morally right and good—well, you are considered insensitive, intolerant, and unloving.

Patience goes deeper. To be patient with others assumes one is in a relationship with them—with all the demands and joys that relationships entail. Patience is not interested in merely coexisting with others.

When I say nothing to the stranger who crowds in front of me in the grocery line, I am being tolerant. I am merely trying to make it possible to get out of the store without creating a scene. But when I say nothing to my hyperactive, nap-deprived five-year-old who does something equally rude, I am being patient. My son is someone I care deeply about, so though I may patiently let his rudeness pass because he happens to be very tired, it's clear that I will not let that sort of behavior continue indefinitely. There will come a point, precisely because I love him, that my patience will run out, and I'll tell him to stop being rude, no matter how tired he is.

Unfortunately, today many have begun to think God is tolerant rather than patient. He's more like a doting grandfather, who long ago stopped caring about the welfare of his grandchildren—having handed the burdensome concerns of love over to his grandchildren's parents. Instead, visits with him are about passing out candy and cuddling. He doesn't worry if these children don't brush their teeth or pick up after themselves or treat each other rudely—he's just the grandpa after all.

To think of God in this way—as merely tolerant—is another way to understand original sin. The Serpent tells Eve that she can just go ahead and eat the forbidden fruit because, after all, God did not mean what he said—"No, you will not die," he says. God is tolerant. He'll understand.

The Bible, however, shows us a different God, a genuinely loving God, a God who is not so much tolerant as patient. He gives a protecting mark to the murderer Cain. He extends the sign of the rainbow over the sky to a world that had forfeited its existence. He rescues a forgetful, idolatrous people from Egypt. He spares a pagan Nineveh. He sends the prophets to warn his people about their wayward ways. He brings them back from exile. He humbly comes in the flesh to the very people he knows will kill him.

Yet notice how each instance of patience is set in a context of judgment, that is, in the context of loving demands that God makes of his people. God is being patient about something he wants these people to become, not tolerant about a people with whom he merely wants to coexist in the universe. His demands are loving demands—not only because they entail love of God and neighbor, but also because to live as God wants is to live in fullness and joy. To live any less, is to live a subhuman existence.

God knows we are ignorant, foolish, shortsighted, rebellious, slothful—you name it. So he is patient. But that patience has a purpose, a destination. God's love may be infinite, but his patience is not.

"The Lord is not slow about his promise, as some think of slowness," says Peter, "but is patient with you, not wanting any to perish, but all to come to repentance." God is not tolerant, not wanting to interfere with our lives. His forbearance has a goal and a limit: "But the day of the Lord will come like a thief, and then the heavens will pass away with a loud noise, and the elements will be dissolved with fire, and the earth and everything that is done on it will be disclosed" (2 Peter 3:9–10).

Paul puts the matter more sternly: "Do you despise the riches of his kindness and forbearance and patience? Do you not realize that God's kindness is meant to lead you to repentance? But by your hard and impenitent heart you are storing up wrath for yourself on the day of wrath, when God's righteous judgment will be revealed" (Rom. 2:4–5).

In this light, we can see that Jesus's impatience with the Pharisees, with the disciples, and with the crowd is a gracious foreshadowing of things to come. Better to endure Jesus's verbal wrath now and repent than not to repent and have to endure the awful day of the Lord. Jesus's impatience is not only a merciful warning, but an invitation: "While God has overlooked the times of human ignorance, now he commands all people everywhere to repent," as Paul tells the Athenians, "because he has fixed a day on which he will have the world judged in righteousness by a man whom he has appointed, and of this he has given assurance to all by raising him from the dead" (Acts 17:30–31).

It seems strange to modern ears to hear that the resurrection is an assurance of the coming judgment of Jesus Christ. But there it is. Thus, there should be no question that the one we're dealing with is not the meek and mild teddy bear of popular faith, the incarnation of the doting grandfather, but the Lord who will come on "clouds, with great power and glory" (Mark 13:26), in those days, as Jesus says, when "the sun will be darkened, and the moon will not give its light, and the stars will be falling from heaven, and the powers in the heavens will be shaken" (Mark 13:24–25).

If this thought is unnerving, so be it. It is the way things are and the way things will be, says Jesus. And those moments when he displays irritation and anger mercifully point to that ultimate reality.

That being said, these brief moments of Jesus's impatience are far outweighed by his lifetime of patience—from the fact of incarnation in the flesh, to forbearance with our ignorance and indifference, to our outright hatred of him on Good Friday. Add to that the slowness of his return as judge. Indeed, Jesus incarnates the God who is "slow to anger and abounding in steadfast love" (Ps. 103:8)—which also can prompt our repentance.

When I was a boy, one of my Saturday chores was to vacuum the house. One Saturday I left early to play baseball with friends, promising my mother that I would be back at a certain time to do my chores. As was sometimes the case, I got wrapped up in the game and found myself trudging home an hour late. As I stepped in the front door, I heard the vacuum going and saw my mother moving it back and forth across the living room carpet.

My heart raced, and I cringed because indeed I deserved her wrath—and my mother was not known for being slow to anger. I prepared for the worst and, over the noise of the vacuum cleaner, shouted, "Mom, I'm sorry I'm late. I'll do the rest."

My mother didn't lift her head and simply said, "That's okay. I'll finish up."

I was stunned. I knew what I deserved—at least a stern lecture, if not more. But my mother showed forbearance, and for that I was grateful. And because I knew it was patience, and not tolerance or indifference, it was many a week before I let that sort of thing happen again.

CHAPTER 14
Harsh Tutors of Love

Then they came to Jerusalem. And he entered the temple and began to drive out those who were selling and those who were buying in the temple, and he overturned the tables of the money changers and the seats of those who sold doves; and he would not allow anyone to carry anything through the temple. He was teaching and saying, "Is it not written, 'My house shall be called a house of prayer for all the nations'? But you have made it a den of robbers."

Mark 11:15–17

Perfect love casts out fear.

1 John 4:18

Patricia Watkins is a minister for Ambassadors for Christ World Outreach Ministries, a Pentecostal church on the South Side of Chicago. She was tired of the violence and drug dealing in the church's neighborhood, so she organized community meetings on the corner of 78th Street and Hermitage Avenue.

The church wanted to reclaim the corner by their presence and their prayers.

People from the church pitched a tent, set up chairs, and started talking about the problems and needs of the block. Some nights thirty people showed up, other nights, many more. Ministers from nearby churches led worship services. Adults tutored children in reading and math. Police and prosecutors came out to support the residents, especially when they marched through the streets shouting, "Whose streets? Our streets!"

One evening as a tent meeting was breaking up, a drug boss ordered his crew back to the streets. It was safe. The cops and most of the preachers were gone. But Watkins had not left, and she didn't like what she was seeing. She confronted the boss.

"Son, do you know why we're out here?" she asked. He shrugged. "We're out here trying to save your life," she continued. "How old are you?"

He said he was seventeen. She replied, "You've got to help us help you."

That's when Watkins says she noticed a car slowly approaching. The driver was looking around nervously. The teenager Watkins had been talking to walked over to the driver. When Watkins realized a drug deal was going on, she grabbed a bullhorn.

"No drugs!" she boomed. "No drugs! No drugs!"

The car sped off, and the young dealer ran—pursued by Watkins, two other pastors, and several women. They chased him for blocks as neighbors on their porches laughed and applauded.

"All we could see was the bottom of his shoes," Watkins later said.

The reporter who wrote about this incident concluded the story by saying, "They did not want to arrest him. They wanted to shame him. They wanted to change him. 'He was our son,' Watkins says."[1]

The phrase that caught my attention was this: "They wanted to shame him." It not only called to mind the many warnings I've heard as a parent, pastor, and teacher against shaming people, it also reminded me of Jesus's behavior.

Jesus would not have been able to get a teaching credential anywhere in the country. He regularly used methods that we are trying ever so hard to eliminate today.

For example, we sometimes find him using shame to motivate: "Those who are ashamed of me and of my words in this adulterous and sinful generation, of them the Son of Man will also be ashamed when he comes in the glory of his Father with the holy angels" (Mark 8:38).

And he sometimes intimidates with threats: "Just as the weeds are collected and burned up with fire, so will it be at the end of the age. The Son of Man will send his angels, and they will collect out of his kingdom all causes of sin and all evildoers, and they will throw them into the furnace of fire, where there will be weeping and gnashing of teeth" (Matt. 13:40–42).

And once Jesus used physical force to make his point: "In the temple he found people selling cattle, sheep, and doves, and the money changers seated at their tables. Making a whip of cords, he drove all of them out of the temple, both the sheep and the cattle. He also poured out the coins of the money changers and overturned their tables" (John 2:14–15).

Not only would Jesus *not* win teacher of the year, he would probably be arrested for assault and battery.

We become more uncomfortable as we look at the details of the incident in the temple. The account begins innocently enough, with people going about the commonplace religious business of buying and selling animals to sacrifice in the temple. A visitor to the scene would have overheard playful teasing amongst family members, hard bargaining between buyers and sellers, local gossip being exchanged, and laughter at the telling of the latest joke, with the lowing of cattle and bleating of sheep and the scent of wool and straw, urine and dung filling the air.

To this very ordinary scene, Jesus reacts viscerally. He doesn't calm himself down with self-talk about patience and longsuffering love or remind himself of the good intentions of these folks—after all, the whole place was designed to facilitate the worship of God. Instead anger rises up like bile—an anger, we should note, he harbors long enough to fashion a whip of cords.

Then suddenly, someone is shouting something about "prayer" and "my Father's house." His face is red; the veins bulge in his neck; his voice rages. The crack of the whip resounds again and again as it stings human skin and animal hide. Sheep scatter in all directions. Cattle bolt and run over people. Everyone panics. There are people running this way and that, sellers reaching for their coins as the whip lashes at their hands, parents desperately grabbing children, someone shouting, "Run. There's a demoniac about!"

The incident remained a vivid memory for the disciples for decades—all four Gospel writers include it in their accounts. If these men wanted to portray only the compassionate Jesus, it would have been rather easy to quietly drop the story. Even Luke and John, known for penning Gospels that portray Jesus in an especially loving light, refuse to leave it out.

But this Jesus is so discomforting some commentators try to cut such passages out of their Bibles.

Jack Nelson-Pallmeyer in his *Is Religion Killing Us? Violence in the Bible and the Quran* writes, "The Gospel writer known as Matthew frequently places threatening and hateful words on the lips of Jesus. . . . Matthew can't seem to imagine people doing the right thing without warnings of violent judgments hanging over their heads, including the threats of hell."[2]

Such exegesis makes us rightfully nervous, but the underlying concern makes sense. We've all been at the receiving end of shame or scare tactics, and we resent it. The methods of religious ideologues are legalistic and oppressive. If we question the politically or religiously correct line, we feel critical eyes staring down at us, silently shaming us. It's even worse if we act out of line—if in a fundamentalist church we begin drinking wine, or if in a liberal church we abstain! Then shame and guilt is ever so subtly laid upon us as our fellow parishioners try to "reeducate" us.

So we struggle with Jesus in such moments because he so willingly employs shame and fear and physical intimidation to motivate people.

A close examination shows that perhaps Jesus knows more about human nature than we do. And our experience confirms Jesus's psychological insights.

Recently I was teasingly griping about my wife to a group of her friends at a church picnic when one of them said, "Don't you ever say anything nice about Barb?" I felt a flood of embarrassment, especially in front of these women, because I pride myself in at least appearing to be a loving husband! But as I thought about the comment later, I realized I had gotten into a bad habit of joking about my wife's flaws and rarely bragging about her many gifts. I immediately set about changing my talk. I was shamed into better behavior.

The young man that Patricia Watkins publicly humiliated was so ashamed, he didn't show his face for three months. But then one night he returned to the tent. He apologized and said he was trying to turn his life around. And he asked Watkins to pray for him.

Shame is a blessed gift sometimes because it can prompt us into better behavior. Fear is a gift as well.

My foster son had been indifferent about religion until he saw the movie *Left Behind* at a friend's house. The movie is about the rapture and God's subsequent judgment. He later asked me if the movie was true. I replied that though Christians differ about the details of the endtimes, we agree on this: Christ will come again, and there will be a judgment. This was a sobering thought for this teenager, and it wasn't long before he committed his life to Christ and was baptized.

Fear, too, can be a blessed gift. And so is physical coercion, which is the reason Christians have respected the authority of government, whose chief agents of justice are its police force and the military. For many Christian theologians the coercion of war is not merely a necessary evil but an act of neighbor love.

When theologian Thomas Aquinas (1225–1274) discusses his views on just war in his *Summa Theologiae* (II–II.40), he does so in the section on the love of God. He reminds us that a peaceful order is not always a just order. We've seen this in recent history in Nazi Germany, which provided peace and order for most of its subjects, but hardly for all. To defend and liberate those being repressed and murdered by a cruel regime, Aquinas argues, is to love them, and that it is positively "meritorious for princes to exercise vindication of justice with zeal against evil people." Reformed theologian John Calvin (1509–1564) also looked at the soldier as an agent of God's love: "Paul meant to refer the precept of respecting power of magistrates to the law of love." Calvin argues in this way because he holds that to soldier justly—that is, to restrain evil out of love for neighbor—is to act in a godly way, because God too restrains evil in his love for us.[3]

Though a minority of Christians have disagreed, most Christians recognize that using physical force is one way to love.

And so the psychology of Jesus seems to suggest that shaming may be loving, and intimidation and physical force may be acts of mercy.

So we seem to be back with shame-based and fear-based religion. And this with a Jesus whom we can assume inspired one of his disciples to write, "Perfect love casts out fear" (1 John 4:18). So how are we to understand Jesus's use of these "negative motivators"?

Here the church father Augustine may be of some help. John Charles Selner's book, *The Teaching of St. Augustine on Fear as a Religious Motive*,[4] summarizes the great fourth-century theologian's insights on fear, which apply across the board. Augustine taught that human beings are designed to love, and the goal of life is to order one's love so that it has a worthy object: God. There are four principal emotions that shape us as we pursue love: *Desire* attracts us to what we love. *Joy* accompanies the experience of love. *Grief* is what we feel when we lose love. *Fear* is the emotion we experience when we believe we may lose love.

Thus fear is far from a negative emotion for Augustine. It is a God-given emotion to prompt us to love truly.

In addition, fear presupposes hope. If we find ourselves in an utterly hopeless situation, in which we believe we are surely doomed, then what we experience is despair. But when we fear, we believe that retaining that which we love is still possible, but we anxiously wonder whether we will retain it.

Thus for Jesus, as for the prophets and for Paul, fear is used to highlight the dire circumstances of living outside of God's will, but the Bible always stops short of instilling despair. To be sure, in some passages the hope is only implicit, as when Jesus castigates the scribes and Pharisees: "Woe to you, scribes and Pharisees, hypocrites!" (Matt. 23:23). Yet even condemnation as severe as this comes with an implied promise: "Repent and you will be forgiven."

Furthermore, fear is a limited tool of love. It can startle us, at least temporarily, to cease from following a wrong desire, but it cannot change the desire. For instance, in a period of anxiety and loneliness, I may be tempted to view pornography as a cheap escape. At times, only the fear of getting caught by my family will stop me from actually viewing it. It will not necessarily erase the illicit desire within me, but it can prevent its fulfillment—at least for a while. As Augustine puts it, a wolf can be frightened away from the sheep pen by the shepherds, but once the shepherds are gone, the wolf will devour the sheep.

So when it comes to eternal matters, Augustine argues that it is useful for Jesus to instill in listeners the fear of judgment and eternal punishment. As Jesus put it, "I tell you, my friends, do not fear those who kill the body, and after that can do nothing more. But I will warn you whom to fear: fear him who, after he has killed, has authority to cast into hell. Yes, I tell you, fear him!" (Luke 12:4–5). As in the case of my foster son, the fear of the judgment can shock someone out of an indifferent adolescent stupor, forcing that person to consider things eternal, especially the mercy of God.

To be motivated merely by fear, however, is to remain in our sins, even if we obey God's law perfectly—because our ultimate desire is not God but to avoid the pain of judgment. This is why the law cannot save. Though it can temporarily prevent us from fulfilling wrong desires, it cannot fill us with the love of God and the desire to please him. Only the grace of God can do that.

The problem with legalistic religion is not the use of fear and shame—all truly religious, truly loving people, like Jesus, employ fear and shame from time to time. The problem is that legalistic religion is shame-*based* and fear-*based*. Fear and shame are the primary tools used to motivate behavior. Love comes in a distant second, if it comes in at all.

The problem with lackadaisical religion is that it completely repudiates fear and assumes there is nothing to be afraid of in this life or the next. Jesus apparently didn't agree, and he regularly told his listeners to fear those things worth fearing—especially the judgment of God. Ironically, a religion without fear, like fear-based religion, has little love because it fails to be honest with people about the real spiritual dangers we face. It is more interested in making people feel good than in helping them.

As Augustine notes, given human nature, fear generally comes before love. To put it positively, fear is the tutor for love. As a tutor, it must eventually leave and make way for the master teacher, love. But this is not something that happens instantaneously. While we are praying to learn to love God for himself, fear can motivate us to break with evil, to correct ourselves, to watch for the enemy, to begin to live the interior life. The closer we grow to Jesus, of course, the more we will be motivated only by love.

Augustine puts it this way: "Perfect charity . . . casteth out fear. Therefore let fear be the beginning. Because the beginning of wisdom is the fear of the Lord. Fear, as it were, prepares a place for charity. But when charity begins to live in us, the fear which prepared a place for it is cast out."[5]

Despite the explanation above, the idea that fear and shame and even physical intimidation can be used for good and loving ends remains an unnerving and frankly dangerous idea. We are wise to be cautious and to use them rarely, and only after getting counsel from others. Indeed, there has been too much abuse in the name of religion. Jesus spews such abusers out of his mouth. The scalpel is an essential tool of healing in the hand of a surgeon, but it can be a dangerous object in the hands of a child or a killer. And the destructiveness of forest fires and arsonists does not stop us from enjoying campfires and fireplaces. Every gift of God is both dangerous and full of potential to bless. Just ask that young man, the former Chicago drug dealer, who finally sought the healing power of Jesus because someone loved him enough to shame him.

CHAPTER 15
The Storm
before the Calm

In those days . . . the sun will be darkened, and the moon
will not give its light; the stars will fall from the sky, and the
heavenly bodies will be shaken. At that time men will see the
Son of Man coming in clouds with great power and glory.

Mark 13:24–26 NIV

And up to the very moment in which I was to become another
man, the nearer the moment approached, the greater horror
did it strike in me.

Augustine[1]

The torment in Augustine's soul that had been building for
years was coming to an awful climax. While hearing a friend
read the story of Antony of the Desert and other early desert
fathers, Augustine recognizes in the purity of their lives the
ugliness of his own. His inability to control his baser passions, especially lust, has been driving him deeper into despair. He now comes face to face with himself and discovers

"how crooked and sordid, bespotted and ulcerous" he is. "I looked and I loathed myself," he writes, "but whither to fly from myself I could not discover."[2]

And so ensues a "vehement quarrel, which I waged with my soul in the chamber of my heart." Later, as "the fiery struggle" rages within, he flees into a garden with his close friend Alypius. "I was greatly disturbed in spirit, angry at myself with a turbulent indignation." In a few moments, he goes into physical convulsions, "Thus I tore my hair, struck my forehead, or, entwining my fingers, clasped my knee."[3]

Then things get worse. "I was sick and tormented, reproaching myself more bitterly than ever," he writes, "rolling and writhing in my chain till it should be utterly broken. By now I was held but slightly, but still was held. And thou, O Lord, didst press upon me in my inmost heart with a severe mercy, redoubling the lashes of fear and shame."[4]

Then the severe mercy turns into a gentle grace. As Augustine is "weeping in the most bitter contrition of my heart," he hears a voice say, "Pick it up, read it; pick it up, read it."

He first thinks it is the voice of children playing nearby. Then he wonders if it might be a divine command to pick up the Bible. So he rushes to the spot where he had left a copy of Paul's letters he had been reading. He opens it, and his eyes fall on Romans 13:13–14: "Let us live honorably as in the day, not in reveling and drunkenness, not in debauchery and licentiousness, not in quarreling and jealousy. Instead, put on the Lord Jesus Christ, and make no provision for the flesh, to gratify its desires."

"I wanted to read no further, nor did I need to," he later recalls. "For instantly, as the sentence ended, there was infused in my heart something like the light of full certainty and all the gloom of doubt vanished away."[5]

A more severe spiritual calamity has not been recorded. It was apocalyptic and unrelenting in its force. As Augustine himself puts it, "Up to the very moment in which I was to become another man, the nearer the moment approached, the greater horror did it strike in me."[6]

In chapter 13 of Mark, Jesus speaks about the historical apocalypse, a time of Augustine-like calamity, but one that will affect the whole planet. "Brother will betray brother to death, and a father his child," says Jesus. "Children will rebel against their parents and have them put to death. All men will hate you because of me, but he who stands firm to the end will be saved" (vv. 12–13 NIV).

To make sure his listeners comprehend the coming cataclysm, Jesus pointedly adds, "Those will be days of distress unequaled from the beginning, when God created the world, until now—and never to be equaled again" (v. 19 NIV).

And to make sure they grasp the gravity of that time, Jesus paints a picture with the most frightening imagery: "But in those days, following that distress, 'the sun will be darkened, and the moon will not give its light; the stars will fall from the sky, and the heavenly bodies will be shaken.' At that time men will see the Son of Man coming in clouds with great power and glory" (vv. 24–26 NIV).

Though the popular proverb tells us to note the calm before the storm, Jesus tells his disciples to pay attention to the storm before the final calm, the eternal Sabbath. The promise is true that, in the end, we will know Jesus as we've never known him before, in glory. But the closer Jesus gets, the more calamity we'll know.

Given the experience of Augustine—and so many others—this seems to be not just the rhythm of history but of life. As Jesus draws near, so rises the storm.

The reasons for the increasing storm are many. When Jesus draws near, he draws near as Lord, and he implicitly challenges all other lords. These lords—greed, lust, ambition, pride, and so forth—do not care to be toppled from their pedestals, and during a crisis, when their lordship is challenged, they will demand ever greater devotion. This, in turn, only aggravates our dis-ease, and we sink deeper than ever into loneliness, guilt, shame, and despair. The closer Jesus gets, the more violent the storm within. It gets to the point that either we must die or Jesus must die, and our souls fight ferociously for self-preservation.

This is what was happening to Augustine. This is what happens to us.

A friend managed to manipulate himself into an adulterous relationship. At first it brought him sexual release, but slowly the guilt and shame mounted. He decided he would put an end to it, but on the very occasion he was going to break up with his lover, he ended up having sex with her. As he drove away, he was plunged into even deeper despair. He drove to a nearby park, shut off the car's engine, and sat there pounding the steering wheel. His guilt and shame were nearly unbearable precisely because Jesus, in his justice and mercy, was approaching.

My friend eventually decided he could not abandon the god of lust on his own, so he confessed to a close friend or two, his brother, a spiritual director, and finally his wife. He wanted others to know of his failure, and he wanted to be held accountable in the future. But before each confession, a new storm raged within: Did he really need to be so vulnerable? Wasn't he already forgiven by God? What would this person think of him? Why not just lay low and move on?

But my friend also knew that Jesus the Healer was drawing near with a healing touch that was also painful to bear.

When Jesus drew near to the epileptic boy, Mark notes that upon seeing Jesus, the evil spirit "convulsed the boy, and he fell on the ground and rolled about, foaming at the mouth" (Mark 8:20). It is a picture of our torment when Jesus draws near to rid us of some evil.

The evil that the epileptic knew was different than the evil that Augustine and my friend experienced. Their evil was brought on by their own sin. The boy, on the other hand, was merely a victim in a fallen world. Nonetheless, the healing presence of Jesus prompts a convulsion in the boy. This, too, is not unusual.

The most common experience of a seizure victim is the convulsion of bitterness. As the just and good and righteous God draws near, it becomes increasingly clear how unjust, how evil, how utterly wasteful is their suffering. We tend to think that victims who wallow in bitterness at God are far from God. Not so. They would not feel so deeply the chasm between their suffering and human wholeness if Truth and Beauty were not close at hand. So in some sense, the more bitter the victim, the closer God likely is.

To be sure, if they are to know peace, they have to release that bitterness at some point. They have to let go of their right to wholeness, abandon the angry attempt to judge God and his ways.

There was no man more bitter than Job, and no man who had more reason to be bitter. He had lost everything—children, wealth, security, and health. So like bile rising from the stomach, Job spits out at God, "Let the day perish in which I was born, and the night that said, 'A man-child is conceived'" (Job 3:3).

Job only knows peace when God, in his merciful majesty, makes himself known to him. "I know that you can do all things," Job finally says to the Lord, "and that no purpose of yours can be thwarted. . . . Therefore I have uttered what I did not understand, things too wonderful for me, which I

161

did not know" (Job 42:2–3). He essentially repents of his bitterness.

Job only sees in a glass darkly, but he instinctively knows that for some reason, he ultimately has no final right to be bitter. In the New Testament, we see more clearly why: God does not permit suffering that he has not been willing to endure himself. To grasp this is to glimpse why the storm before the calm is finally good news.

To understand this, we need to make some comparisons. We tend to think that the greatest of injustices are perpetrated against infants and children. Nothing compels righteous indignation more than learning that children have been beaten, sexually abused, or slaughtered. There is no greater tragedy, we say.

Let us set aside for the moment the doctrine of original sin, which would suggest that no one, not even an infant, is utterly innocent. Be that as it may, the innocence that we perceive in babies is finally a passive innocence. They are too young to be responsible moral agents. So they are innocent by default.

Jesus was as innocent as we perceive a babe to be. He was sinless. He was pure. He was untainted by the world. The difference is this: he was a responsible moral agent. His innocence was not a passive innocence but the result of his freedom. His innocence was active. Yet this is the Jesus who was arrested, tried, beaten, and killed.

Now add to this moral incongruity the knowledge that this one was holy God incarnate; he was true righteousness, true justice, true love. Not only was he innocent, but he deserved nothing less than worship, honor, glory, and obeisance.

Yet the innocent and holy one was mocked, beaten, and murdered by ungrateful, stubborn, malicious people. *Injustice* is hardly a big enough word to describe the enormity of the moral incongruity. *Blasphemy* gets closer. No other injustice in the history of humankind compares.

As this injustice drew near, Jesus recognized it for what it was, and its enormity absolutely frightened him. He begged his Father to let it pass by him. He sweated blood in agony over it. The movie *The Passion of the Christ* is criticized for exaggerating the physical and psychological sufferings of Jesus. The movie is indeed unnerving in this respect. But in theological fact, the movie cannot even approximate the actual suffering of and injustice perpetrated against Jesus.

At the same time, this movie—and all other literature and media combined—have only been able to hint at the glory that came three days later. Popular author and speaker Tony Campolo is famous for, among other things, a talk he gave called, "It's Friday, but Sunday's Coming." The sermon hinged on the notion that despite the suffering we endure, the resurrection is coming soon on its heels, and the moment we cry out that God has utterly forsaken us is the very moment when he is drawing near.

What we discover in Holy Week is that, indeed, Jesus is able to sympathize with our weakness—whether it be from sin or unjust suffering—because he has been tempted as we are. He knows the writhing agony that comes just before the glorious power and presence of God is made known.

Once again we discover a harder truth about life in Christ. We promise people peace and joy in Christ, and this is a sound promise. We assure people that they can know Jesus personally. That assurance is sure. But we often fail to tell them about the calamity that comes to the one who seeks to know, really know, Jesus—the real Jesus.

Really knowing the real Jesus is a glorious thing, and it's something we grow into in this life and for eternity. But we can easily get confused along the way. Those who want nothing less than to be unified with Love need to realize what that entails. And those who know calamities and agonies, physical and spiritual, should never despair. Because the Lord you want to love, the peace you want so desperately to know, and the justice you demand is drawing near, just at the hour when things seem their worst.

CHAPTER 16
Forsaken by Grace

My God, my God, why have you forsaken me?

Mark 15:34

We are fonder of consolations than we are of the cross.

Teresa of Avila[1]

Just when we need him most, God forsakes us.

Given the context of Jesus's agonizing cry from the cross—a plaintive cry at the hour of death, with silence as its only answer—one can draw few other conclusions about what this incident teaches. At the hour of desperation, God is absent.

This is a disturbing thought, so it's not the theme of sermons or inspirational books. It's not the truth we highlight when marketing the gospel to seekers. But it is the truth of human experience. We would do well to acknowledge it up front.

We experience God's absence in a variety of ways. At one end of the spectrum is an excruciating absence. Here the absence is palpable because God's presence is so desperately needed. It is the experience of Jesus on the cross. It is our experience.

A couple conceives a child. There are complications in the pregnancy. Visits to specialists. Tests. More tests. Then horrific news.

"We have some problems," the doctor announces. "The fetus has a malformed heart—the aorta is attached incorrectly. There are missing portions of the cerebellum. A club foot. A cleft palate and perhaps a cleft lip. Possibly spina bifida. This is probably a case of Trisomy 13 or Trisomy 18. In either case, it is a condition incompatible with life."

The couple is stunned into silence.

"It's likely the fetus will spontaneously miscarry," the doctor continues. "If the child is born, it will not survive long outside the womb. You need to decide if you want to try to carry this pregnancy to term."

The couple knew what the doctor was suggesting, but this was not an option for them. And so the long wait for the birth, months of anticipation of the agony of witnessing a few desperate minutes with their son. And then the hollowing out of the heart. An emptiness. Grief. And the question, "Where are you God?"[2]

The absence of God is known not just in the privacy of our lives but also across the stretch of history. It does not take a vivid imagination for the mind to ponder Nazi death ovens or corpses piled high in Rwandan villages. And all the while we ask, "Where were you, God?"

By God's grace, the horrific is held in check. Many potential catastrophes are miraculously averted. Many sufferers know divine visitations in their hour of crisis. But these exceptions don't negate the reality that people experience God's absence in such times.

Most of us, however, know only the day-to-day absence. We are functional atheists most of the time. We jump out of bed, gulp down coffee, and sprint into the day, immersing ourselves in all its petty and large concerns. We barely give God a thought and pretty much live our days as if he is away on a trip. This sense of absence does not produce a crisis. In fact, on most days we prefer this type of life because God is not around to interrupt our busy schedules.

Sometimes, of course, we get in a spiritual mood, and we seek to practice the presence of God moment by moment. Even then, we find no unambiguous signs of his presence: no burning bushes, no shimmering clouds, no undisputed miracles, no voices from heaven. We are tempted to chalk up deeply mystical experiences to chemical reactions in the brain or psychological disturbances of a troubled soul.

Indeed—so as not to overstate the case—people of all times have experienced something beyond themselves, something beyond physical reality, and something or someone utterly powerful, mysterious, and even loving.

This is certainly true of the new Christian. There is no question that in the early months or years of walking with Christ, many know a spiritual presence as real as the food they eat and the air they breathe. But it is also the common experience of Christians, as they get older in the faith, to find God missing more and more. They turn to speak to the loving companion with whom they have been freshly walking, but it seems they are talking to the air.

Sometimes this is due to a slow hardening of the heart in which pride and self-seeking make it impossible to know God's presence. But this sense of absence can be found in the most devout of saints, like Mother Teresa. Her journals reveal something remarkable: while the world marveled at her devotion to Christ and the poor—while she was incarnating the very love and presence of God in the world—she was experiencing frightening spiritual emptiness, a sense that God had utterly abandoned her. "Lord, my God, who am I that You should forsake me?" she wrote. "I call, I cling, I want, and there is no one to answer."[3]

It is not an uncommon experience, then, among sinners and saints, to discover that God is nowhere to be found. It is also a common experience that this happens just when we need him most. This abandonment—in fact, the constellation of absence experienced through all time and space, from the mundane to the horrific—is what Jesus experienced on the cross. His cry is our cry.

Fortunately, this is not only the truth of human experience, it is also the beginning of the good news of the gospel.

The absence of God is good news, first, because it signals that he desires a genuine, mutual relationship. "If we could mechanically draw him into an encounter, force him to meet us, simply because we have chosen this moment to meet him," writes Anthony Bloom in his classic, *Beginning to Pray*, "there would be no relationship and no encounter. We can do that with an image, with the imagination, or with the various idols we can put in front of us instead of God; we can do nothing of the sort with the living God, any more than we can do it with a living person. A relationship must begin and develop in mutual freedom."[4]

When my wife and I fell in love in college, we longed desperately to spend time together. We arrived at weekly Bible study early to talk, sat next to each other, and then stayed afterwards late into the night. We ate together in the cafeteria, we played on the same softball team, we took classes together, and we wrote term papers together.

We relished this—for a time. Then claustrophobia began to set in. Though both of us felt it, we didn't feel free to speak of it. I worried what she would think if I said I wanted some time alone. She wondered the same. We didn't want to hurt each other, but slowly we both felt increasingly trapped. It wasn't until we could admit we wanted to be apart that we had a relationship built on confidence and freedom.

The analogy with God is imperfect. First, despite the picture drawn above, God is never absent from our lives. The universe is full of his glory, and there is no corner of the universe where he is not present. So the sense of forsakenness is, in fact, something that God has to manufacture, an experience he has to take special pains to create. If he left things to themselves, we would always know the utter immediacy and nearness of God.

In addition, we can never feel claustrophobic in the presence of infinite love and infinite freedom. The closer we get to God, the more freedom we experience.

Still, the relational dynamics—the ebb and flow of intimacy, the give and take of love—are very much necessary in a relationship with God. Claustrophobia may not be the reason God withdraws the sense of his presence, but the rhythm of a relationship with God includes times when he doesn't seem near—for reasons we'll explore in a bit.

We need to put this whole matter in perspective, however. "If you look at the relationship in terms of *mutual* relationship, you will see that God could complain about us a great deal more than we about him," writes Bloom. "We complain that he does not make himself present to us for the few minutes we reserve for him, but what about those twenty-three and a half hours during which God may be knocking at our door and we answer 'I am busy, I am sorry' or when we do not answer at all because we do not even hear the knock at the door of our heart, of our minds, of our conscience, of our life."[5]

Humility also requires that we recognize the childish pride hidden in our breasts when we demand God's presence. How different this is from the picture we see in the Bible when people suddenly find themselves in the presence of the divine. When, after the miracle of the catch of fish, Peter recognizes who Jesus is, he says, "Go away from me, Lord, for I am a sinful man" (see Luke 5:1–11). When the centurion needs Jesus to heal his servant, he entreats him not to come into his home because he is unworthy to receive one so great and so holy (see Matt. 8:5–14). For such people, to be in the presence of

God was not a right but a privilege, and something they knew they didn't deserve.

We indeed have a relationship with God, but that relationship cannot deepen—we cannot know God's presence—if we treat him as an equal or, even worse, as a servant of our every spiritual whim who must be available to us on demand. The relationship may be mutual, but it needs to be grounded in the reality of who is relating to whom. When we get that wrong, no wonder we experience God's absence, for we are no longer seeking after the true God—the holy and glorious Creator of heaven and earth—but a mirror of our spiritual egos. We are doing nothing more than shouting into the empty vacuum of the self, and we are only hearing the echo of our own whiny voice.

This brings us to the second bit of good news found in the absence of God: it is one of the ways God topples our idols.

At some point—usually at many points—a child needs to replace the false image he has of his parents. That false image usually consists of this: parents are wonderful, loving people who are anxious to meet my every need. The child has the first part right, but the second does not follow. Thus, requests turn into demands, and when demands aren't met, a tantrum follows. The parents know well what is going on, and the truly loving parent will simply not respond. Parents may even physically separate themselves, confining the child to his or her room, giving a "time out" until the child can calm down. Parents "abandon" the child because they want to have a healthy, loving relationship with him or her. To have such a relationship, the child must understand who those parents really are—not servants of the child's whim.

Too often, we do not want the true God as much as we want the god of our imaginations, the god who wants nothing more than to make us happy. This god wants to affirm us as his beloved children, and so he would never drive us into a wilderness. He does not demand repentance but instead tells us to accent the positive in our lives. When we do need a course correction (we're human, after all), he never scolds us but only speaks kindly. And he doesn't even do that much, because, well, he's infinitely patient. In the end, he's not so much interested in making us holy as helping us be nice, not so much concerned about our character as in our feeling good about ourselves, not so much helping us know Christ's sufferings as enabling us to live an upbeat life. And he is a god who never, ever forsakes us, and certainly not in a time of trouble.

Unfortunately, this idol is the very one the Jesus of Mark's Gospel works to topple—and Jesus' sense of forsakenness on the cross is the exclamation point of this message. Jesus shows us a God mean and wild who shocks us by refusing, absolutely, to conform to our sentimental image of him.

Perhaps the greatest danger—and the most tempting idol—is to imagine that God is the servant of our desires, who meets all our needs and is there for us in crises in exactly the way we need him to be there for us. But this idol is built on a false base, as if our desires are the measure of what is best for us, as if our "needs" are really our deepest needs, as if the only and best way to resolve a crisis is to do so in the way we think it should be resolved—as if we were all-wise, all-knowing, and all-loving.

The rude awakening that happens as a result of God's abandonment forces us to consider that perhaps there is Another who knows what we really desire, understands what we really need, and fathoms how best to help us in the hour of crisis. But before we can meet the true God, the false god must be abandoned. If we will not abandon it, God in his grace will destroy it for us. And between the time of that destruction and the time when the true God reenters our lives, it will feel as if God has forsaken us.

The good news of the sense of God's abandonment has another dimension still. This one is revealed by those whom we commonly call saints. Saints are saints in part because they want to know Christ as profoundly as is humanly possible. One of the first saints, the apostle Paul, put it this way: "I want to know Christ and the power of his resurrection and the sharing of his sufferings by becoming like him in his death" (Phil. 3:10).

Saints are really sinners on spiritual steroids. They are people like you and me, people who want to know Christ more and more. The difference is that they are much more willing than the rest of us to do what it takes to know Christ.

They want to know Christ in his holiness. They want to know him in his power. They want to know his love. They want to know him in his glory. So far so good, we say.

Saints want to know Jesus completely and love him fully, and that means they want to know him in his humiliation. They want to know the Christ who is deserted by the disciples and abandoned by the Father. They want to know not just the resurrection but also the sufferings.

It is a common expression in some Christian quarters to say, "I want to have the heart of God." The common meaning is, "I want to feel the love and compassion God has for all people." But to have the heart of God—if we really want that—means to feel the brokenness of God as he looks at his creation.

Another sentiment of the Christian life: "I want to be more godly." Another still: "I want to imitate Christ." And on it goes. Nearly every expression begins with the notion that we want to be like Christ, live as he lived, see the world from his perspective. But what we don't usually consider is that living that life means knowing an uncommon grief.

If once from the cross Christ screams, "My God, my God, why have you forsaken me?" how many times has God lamented, "O man, O woman, why have you forsaken me?"

The Old Testament is filled with this theme. We can hardly turn a page before we see another instance of the people of

God deserting their Creator and God's grieving and, yes, sometimes angry response. It is expressed no better than in the book of Hosea:

> When Israel was a child, I loved him,
>   and out of Egypt I called my son.
> The more I called them,
>   the more they went from me;
> they kept sacrificing to the Baals,
>   and offering incense to idols.
> Yet it was I who taught Ephraim to walk,
>   I took them up in my arms;
>   but they did not know that I healed them.
> I led them with cords of human kindness,
>   with bands of love.
> I was to them like those
>   who lift infants to their cheeks.
> I bent down to them and fed them.
>
> Hosea 11:1–4

To know God—to be godly in the deepest sense—is to know the suffering of God, the utter grief he knows because of our abandoning him. This is, in part, what Christ experienced on the cross—the abandonment of all. It is what we must experience if we are to know Christ intimately and to be like Christ. It is what we must experience if we are to truly understand, at a place deep in our souls, the measure of God's love for us.

A simple analogy will do. Though children experience something of the love of their parents as they grow up, they will never understand the depth of their parents' love until they become parents themselves. Then the grown children are able to see with the heart of their parents. Then they know, among other things, the sacrifices and heartache of their parents and the measure of their parents' love for them.

In a mysterious process, the Father makes it possible for us to know what it is like to love as he loves. It comes paradoxically as we experience like Christ the abandonment of all love, as we come to know the sufferings of Christ.

To know Christ's sufferings, however, is not just an exercise in identifying with God or "feeling" as God feels. It is also something we must experience if we are to love as Christ did. The world is a broken, grieving place. And given the human condition—our basic hardness of heart—we cannot truly love it until we experience that brokenness.

Again, a common experience can illustrate this. For most of my life, I have been dutifully empathetic when someone told me of their tribulations taking care of an aging parent. I'm sure I communicated a certain level of concern. Then my aging father slowly developed dementia and Parkinson's. The loss of memory along with the loss of physical control is a one-two punch of immeasurable sadness. There comes no more poignant moment for a son than when he has to feed his father, just as the father fed him decades earlier.

It took that suffering for me to have genuine empathy for people whose parents' minds and bodies are slowly, inexorably deteriorating. It is an empathy that is able to express itself now with sincerity and with the offer of help that is no longer mere gesture.

How much more will we be able to love if we experience Christ's suffering—especially his sense of utter abandonment on the cross? Indeed, God forsakes us just when we need him most. But it is all about love: the casting down of our sentimental idols and the lifting up of the true God, the God who loves us so much that he allows us to share in his grief and to be instruments of his merciful love.

CHAPTER 17
Fearsome
Love

So they went out and fled from the tomb, for terror and amazement had seized them; and they said nothing to anyone, for they were afraid.

Mark 16:8

Once in Israel love came to us incarnate, stood in the doorway between two worlds, and we were all afraid.

Annie Dillard[1]

There comes a time in the life of faith when Jesus must die. For many people, the Christ who dies is an amalgam of their fantasies and our culture's fancies. In our time, that often means this: Jesus is the nicest person we can imagine. He is a kindergarten teacher of a humanity that is as vulnerable as a group of five-year-olds. So, of course, he does not raise his voice. He affirms and reaffirms our fragile self-esteem. We may paint an awful picture with the sinfulness of our lives, but we needn't worry. Remember? Jesus refused to lift a rock of judgment against the woman caught in adultery. So, like the nonjudgmental teacher, he simply asks, "So, tell me about this painting, this life of yours," and without pressure lets us figure out on our own how we might improve.

This Jesus puzzles us, of course. He seems so nice; we can't imagine why he doesn't answer all our prayers or why he allows evil to run free. Consequently, we have our doubts, like everyone else in this age, wondering how a congenial Lord can be, well, so inattentive. Maybe he's not really in charge after all. Then suddenly our faith is bolstered by an inspirational best seller about the best life or the purpose-driven life or the border-expanding life, and we're ready to be patient with Jesus a little longer—as long as he keeps us feeling good about ourselves and optimistic about tomorrow.

Hyperbole to be sure, but not all that unlike my imagination some days. This Jesus may be a comfort, but in the end he is a bore. He is the product of our culture's paltry imagination. He is a Jesus without substance, a mere shadow of the Jesus who roamed the hills of Galilee.

When our imaginary Jesus dies, most of us do not have the courage to up and quit the faith. We have too much of our identity invested in it. People like me want at least to honor Jesus. Like the women who came to Jesus's tomb (Mark 16:1), we still want to carry spices there and anoint him. He may be irrelevant and as good as dead now, but he was a great man in his day. And his legacy—my gosh!

Some brands of the faith are more susceptible to this religious path. The liturgically minded—Anglicans like myself—can make do with this sort of faith for decades. We say the historic prayers, remember the noble saints, and honor Jesus with all the smells and bells that money can buy. It is a glorious tradition.

After I left the pastorate, I slowly descended into a spiritual funk. I wasn't a complete pagan or an utter hypocrite. And, yes, praying the Anglican liturgy week after week helped me maintain the little bit of vibrant faith I had. But a lot of the time, I was merely going to anoint a dead body with spices, to honor a God who simply didn't make sense anymore. There was no vibrancy in prayer. Scripture felt repetitive. Theology and spiritual writings had little meaning.

That's because the Christ I had fashioned in my image had died. It wasn't the Jesus our culture honors, but it was a figment of my imagination nonetheless. At some point, I had to realize that all the anointing and the spices in the world weren't going to bring this Jesus back to life.

"Do not be alarmed," says the angel. "You are looking for Jesus of Nazareth, who was crucified. He has been raised; he is not here. . . . He is going ahead of you in Galilee; there you will see him" (Mark 16:6).

The first step in finding the real Jesus is to recognize that he is not here, he is not in one's life as he should be. He is gone. It is to realize that we have been following a fake Jesus, a charlatan, an imposter. And that imposter is as good as dead. The real Jesus is long gone and waiting for us in Galilee.

Galilee is the beginning of things. Galilee is where Jesus was first revealed to us. Galilee is where we must go to get in touch with reality again.

To go to Galilee means to remember what it was about Jesus that first connected with you. It means to explore those things that drew you into the faith in the first place. This Jesus likely left you with more questions than answers and perplexed you as much as fulfilled you. It took years to get all those answers and resolve those perplexities and thus years to refashion him in your image. Instead, return to the alluring, mysterious, captivating Jesus who first attracted you—not in a naïve way (as if you've learned nothing), but in a way that sees the simplicity of Jesus within the complexity of faith.

To go to Galilee also means to look once again, with freshness and honesty, at Jesus when he walked the Galilean countryside.

It means, quite simply, to reacquaint yourself with the Jesus of the Gospels. Whenever I've been in a spiritual funk, this has been the way I've reacquainted myself with the real Jesus.

This book has been an attempt to do that regarding some larger issues facing twenty-first-century North American Christianity. I've tried to give focused attention to neglected words and actions of Jesus, to visit sites in his Galilean ministry that we are apt to overlook, but places where a full-orbed, dynamic Jesus is to be found.

Those accustomed to Jesus meek and mild will be frightened by Jesus mean and wild. And perhaps they have already quit reading long ago. But what I've discovered time and again is that the "mean" Jesus is more merciful than the mild one, and the wild Jesus is more fascinating than the mild one.

Indeed, the basic notion prevailing about Jesus—that he is loving, merciful, and kind—is right on the mark. C. S. Lewis says that every age gets something right and something wrong about God. This is something our age has gotten right. What we have failed to see is how dynamic, how free, how surprising, how untamable, how paradoxical this love is.

This love is a grace that demands repentance, a balm that can hurt, an impatience that has a merciful end, a suffering that redeems. Paul has said, "Note then the kindness and severity of God" (Rom. 11:22). If nothing else, this book has been an attempt to return to Galilee and discover that these are not two contradictory aspects of God's character but one and the same.

It's a funny way to end a gospel of Good News, but there it is: "So they went out and fled from the tomb, for terror and amazement had seized them; and they said nothing to anyone, for they were afraid" (Mark 16:8).

Half Dome is a mass of granite that majestically overlooks Yosemite Valley. It is a "dome" that a glacier sliced in half as it cut through the tons of granite on its way to creating one of the most captivating scenes of all creation.

You can scale the one kilometer face of Half Dome if you're a rock climber, or you can hike to its top. Or you can drive to Glacier Point and behold it face to face, as it were, across the Yosemite Valley. After driving to 8,800 feet, you get out of your car and view one of the world's wonders. The overwhelming amount of granite alone causes one's chest to freeze. Add to that the sweeping panorama of Yosemite Valley and beyond, and then the sheer drop from Glacier Point into the valley—it fills one with a combination of awe and fear. Awe at the majesty of the scene; fear knowing that a misstep near the edge means certain death. The fear does not take away from the magnificence but instead makes it all that more magnificent. In fact, only fools would not have a healthy fear. And thus most spectators view it in silence or communicate only in quiet whispers. It is a holy and sobering moment to see such grandeur.

Our culture would have us put our faith in a Jesus who is a mere bed of carnations. Interesting. Pretty. He adds color and fragrance to life and little more. Jesus, according to Mark's Gospel, is Half Dome. The vision of the true Jesus compels reverence, silence, and yes, fear.

Fear is not a euphemism for awe—though it includes awe. This fear is genuine for the women at the tomb and for us because in meeting the resurrected Jesus, we stand on the precipice of life and death. We should be afraid—as we are afraid of the edge of Glacier Point. But we are nonetheless drawn near to the very thing that can hasten our death if we are not careful. We are sane to be afraid. And we would be fools not to draw closer.

One final thing needs to be said about this passage and the theme of this book. We have noted time and again how in many ways the Jesus of Galilee is foreign to our religious sensibilities—so strange we hardly recognize him. We have explored the elusive character of God and how at times he even withdraws the sense of his presence from us. But we have also noted how the omnipresent God cannot but be present to us at all times and all places. We have to turn to another Gospel to unlock this paradox (as far as a paradox can be unlocked).

At the end of the Gospel of Luke, the resurrected Jesus meets two disciples walking toward Emmaus. They are disconsolate at the recent turn of events, and they spill out their grief to their new companion. But Jesus, as elusive as ever, remains hidden, even though they spend hours with him, talking about recent events, about Scripture, about prophecy, and about the Christ!

As the evening wears on, the disciples invite the stranger to dine with them. Then Luke notes this: "When he was at the table with them, he took bread, blessed and broke it, and gave it to them. Then their eyes were opened, and they recognized him" (Luke 24:30–31). And to make sure we've gotten the point, Luke summarizes their retelling of the incident to the other disciples like this: "Then they told what had happened on the road, and how he had been made known to them in the breaking of the bread" (Luke 24:35).

This is clearly an allusion to the Eucharist, reinforcing its importance to early Christians. But it also points to another reality—how God is both hidden and revealed in his creation.

God has not only blessed the created order by calling it good (Gen. 1), but he has also infused it with his glory:

> The heavens are telling the glory of God;
>   and the firmament proclaims his handiwork.
> Day to day pours forth speech,
>   and night to night declares knowledge.
> There is no speech, nor are there words;
>   their voice is not heard;
> yet their voice goes out through all the earth,
>   and their words to the end of the world.
>
> Psalm 19:1–4

He has blessed his creation and made it a vehicle of revelation, the most complete of which he accomplished by taking on flesh and rising from the dead in bodily form. Without eyes to see, creation looks like mere nature, a patchwork of living organisms and geological forms. With the eyes of faith, we see something else. As St. Francis put it in his famous "Canticle of Brother Sun":

> Praised be You, my Lord, with all your creatures,
>   especially Sir Brother Sun,
> Who is the day and through whom You give us light.
> And he is beautiful and radiant with great splendor;
>   and bears a likeness of You, Most high One.[2]

We so wish to encounter God directly, with an unmediated revelation, to know him directly, unambiguously, with unbrokered intimacy—but there is no such knowing. God has chosen to reveal himself through the physical creation. Even a voice from heaven has to pass through the ear canal via sound waves. A miracle is witnessed with eyes that depend on light waves. An inner thought or feeling or dream comes by way of electrical-chemical impulses in the brain. It is paper and ink and abstract symbols—Scripture—working through electrical impulses in the brain (called thoughts) that become a chief way in which God comes to us. It is the church, full of flesh-and-blood sinners, that is the body of Christ in the world today.

This elusive God can very well be missed by the skeptic. Visions become psychological delusions, Scripture the myths of ancient people, the church just another voluntary society. But those with eyes to see know that Jesus—the flesh-and-blood God who rose bodily—makes himself known concretely in the mundane things of this world.

God is found in the magnificence of Half Dome and in the miracle of the embryo, in the abandoned play of children, in intimate conversation over coffee. He is found when a hus-

181

band and wife make love or when two or three are gathered in his name. He is found in the hungry, in the homeless, in the prisoners. And most specially, he is found in his Word, in his body, and in the breaking of bread and the sharing of wine in his name. Belden Lane writes, "God disguises himself, hiding in a manger, his majesty veiled upon a cross, so that we might irresistibly be drawn to a grace far closer than we ever imagined."[3]

Half Dome moments, resurrection moments, when heaven and earth fuse, when suddenly we recognize the presence of the glorious Christ—such moments make us gasp, stare, whisper, and tremble. We are in the presence of something both dangerous and wonderful.

We'll be tempted to run—both from it in fear and toward it in fascination. We want to shout the news to everyone we meet, and yet, like the women at the tomb, we're afraid to utter a word lest people think we've gone mad. For Jesus has come to us, the real Jesus—mean, wild, and pulsing with an unnerving and irresistible love.

NOTES

Introduction

1. Stephen Prothero, in an online interview, OnReligion.com, Saturday, January 24, 2004, http://www.onreligion.com/article.php?story=20040124100634164.

2. Annie Dillard, "Expedition to the Pole," in *Teaching a Stone to Talk: Expeditions and Encounters* (New York: Harper & Row, 1982), 40.

3. "There's No Solving Mystery of Christ," *Chicago Sun-Times*, January 16, 2004, http://www.suntimes.com/index/.

Chapter 1: Difficult Love

1. Tom Downey, "Hazing and Heroism," *New York Times*, January 9, 2004, http://www.nytimes.com/.

2. Athanasius, *Life of St. Antony and Letter to Marcellinus* (Mahwah, NJ: Paulist Press, 1980), 38.

3. Aleksandr I. Solzhenitsyn, *The Gulag Archipelago 1918–1956: An Experiment in Literary Investigation* (New York: Harper & Row, 1973), 18–19.

4. Ibid., 614–15.

5. Ibid., 610–11.

6. This quotation and those in the following four paragraphs are taken from Downey, "Hazing and Heroism."

Chapter 2: A Hopeful Repentance

1. St. Isaac of Syria, *Isaac, Bishop of Nineveh: The Ascetical Homilies of Saint Isaac the Syrian*, trans. Holy Transfiguration Monastery (Brookline, MA: Holy Transfiguration Monastery, 1984).

2. *The Book of Common Prayer and Administration of the Sacraments and Other Rites and Ceremonies of the Church* (New York: Oxford University Press, 1928), 6.

3. E. A. Wallis Budge, ed. and trans., *The Paradise of the Holy Fathers*, vol. 2, (Seattle, WA: St. Nectarios Press, 1984), http://www.innerlightproductions.com/thoughts/dec0797.htm.

4. Quotations in this and the following paragraph are from Eugene Peterson, *A Long Obedience in the Same Direction: Discipleship in an Instant Society* (Downers Grove, IL: InterVarsity, 1980), 25.

5. Ambrose, *Concerning Repentance, Book 2*, from *Some of the Principle Works of St. Ambrose*, trans. H. de Romestin, in Nicene and Post-Nicene Fathers, Second Series vol. 10, ed. Philip Schaff and Henry Wace (1896; repr., Peabody, MA: Hendrickson, 1999), 345.

6. Frederica Mathewes-Green, "Whatever Happened to Repentance?" *Christianity Today*, February 4, 2002, 56.

7. Quotations in this and the following paragraph are from Cyril, archbishop of Jerusalem, Second Catechetical Lecture, "On Repentance, the Remission of Sin, and the Adversary," in *The Works of Saint Cyril of Jerusalem*, vol. 1, trans. Leo P. McCauley, in the series The Fathers of the Church, vol. 61 (Washington, DC: Catholic University of America Press, 1968), 99.

Chapter 3: Holy War

1. Sr. Benedicta Ward, *The Sayings of the Desert Fathers* (Kalamazoo, MI: Cistercian Publications, 1975), 89.

2. Quotations in this and the following four paragraphs are from Jim Wilkins, "D-Day Recollections," The Queen's Own Rifles of Canada, http://users.erols.com/wolfy/qor/html/body_wilkins.html.

3. Ernst Käseman, *Jesus Means Freedom* (Philadelphia: Fortress Press, 1969), 58.

4. Augustine, *Confessions*, book 8, 5:10, 11:26, from *Confessions and Enchiridion*, trans. and ed. Albert C. Outler (1955). Digitized by Harry Plantinga, 1993, http://www.fordham.edu/halsall/basis/confessions-bod.html.

5. Hudson Taylor, *China: Its Spiritual Needs and Claims*, 7th ed. (London: Morgan & Scott, 1887), as found in *Christian History: Hudson Taylor* 52 (1992): 13.

6. Quotations in this and the following two paragraphs are from Roger Steer, "Pushing Inward," *Christian History: Hudson Taylor* 52 (1992): 13–14.

7. Ibid.

8. From *Paradise of the Desert Fathers*. This is not a single book but a collection of sayings and accounts written by and about the Desert Fathers of Egypt. This and other excerpts can be found on the Copt Net website, originally from a book by Dr. Benedicta Ward, http://www.coptic.net/articles/ParadiseOfDesertFathers.txt.

Chapter 4: Prayer Scandals

1. Adapted from *The Book of Common Prayer and Administration of the Sacraments and Other Rites and Ceremonies of the Church* (New York: The Church Hymnal Corporation, 1979), 832.

2. Quotations in this and the following paragraph in the text are from Saint Bonaventure, "The Major Legend of Saint Francis," chap. 3 in *Francis of Assisi: Early Documents*, vol. 2, *The Founder*, ed. Regis J. Armstrong, J. A. Hellmann, and William J. Short (New York: New City Press, 2000), 542.

3. Julian of Norwich, *Revelations of Divine Love*, trans. John Skinner (New York: Image, 1997), 22.

4. W. J. Townsend, *Robert Morrison: The Pioneer of Chinese Missions* (London: S.W. Partridge, 1891), 54.

Chapter 5: It's Not Nice to Be Nice

1. Augustine, *City of God*, trans. Henry Bettenson (1972; repr., New York: Penguin, 2004), bk. 9, chap. 5, 349.

2. "I Sing a Song of the Saints of God," by Lesbia Scott from *Rejoice in the Lord: A Hymn Companion to the Scriptures*, ed. Erik Routley (Grand Rapids: Eerdmans, 1985), number 401.

3. Catherine of Siena, *The Dialogue of Saint Catherine of Siena*, trans. Algar Thorold (London: Kegan Paul, Trench, Trubner and Co., 1907). Digitized by Harry Plantinga, 1994, http://www.ccel.org/c/catherine/dialog/cache/dialog.txt.

4. Quotations in this and the following paragraph are from Sigrid Undset, *Catherine of Siena*, trans. Kate Austin-Lund (New York: Sheed and Ward, 1953), 184.

5. Marilyn Chandler McEntyre, "Nice Is Not the Point," *Christianity Today*, November 13, 2000, 104.

6. Ben Witherington III, *The Gospel of Mark: A Socio-Rhetorical Commentary* (Grand Rapids: Eerdmans, 2001), 104.

7. Peterson, *Long Obedience in the Same Direction*, 127.

8. Witherington, *Gospel of Mark*, 139.

Chapter 6: Love That Makes Enemies

1. A saying Truman used often, in one variation or another, probably beginning in 1948, according to David H. Stowe, deputy to the assistant to Truman and then Truman's administrative assistant. See Truman Presidential Museum and Library website, http://www.trumanlibrary.org/oralhist/stowe3.htm.

2. Many biographies tell this story, but a succinct one can be found in Don Attwater, *St. John Chrysostom: Preacher and Pastor* (London: Harvill Press, 1939), especially chap. 3, and 5–10.

3. Charles Finney, "Blessed Are the Persecuted," *Oberlin Evangelist*, September 15, 1858, published at Gospel Truth, http://www.gospeltruth.net/1858OE/580915_persecuted_blesse.htm.

4. Joel Marcus, *Mark 1–8: A New Translation with Introduction and Commentary* (New York: Doubleday, 2000), 252.

5. Peterson, *Long Obedience in the Same Direction*, 123.

6. Jonathan Taylor, "Smuggling Cats for a Gay Celebrity," *Christianity Today*, October 2004, 94.

Chapter 7: Wretched Individualism

1. Richard Lamb, *The Pursuit of God in the Company of Friends* (Downers Grove, IL: InterVarsity, 2003), 17.

2. The story of Francis of Assisi is condensed from the opening chapters of my book, Mark Galli, *Francis of Assisi and His World* (Oxford: Lion, 2002). The main sources for

that book include primary material found in Regis J. Armstrong, ed., *Francis of Assisi: Early Documents: The Saint* (Hyde Park, NY: New City, 1999), Regis J. Armstrong, ed., *Francis of Assisi: Early Documents: The Founder I* (Hyde Park, NY: New City, 2000), as well as secondary sources such as Omer Englebert, *St. Francis of Assisi: A Biography* (Chicago: Franciscan Herald Press, 1965), and Adrian House, *Francis of Assisi: A Revolutionary Life* (New York: Hidden Springs, 2000, 2001), among others.

Chapter 8: Good Warnings

1. Michael Elliot, "Sea of Sorrow," *Time*, January 10, 2005, http://www.time.com/time/.
2. Ibid.
3. Simone Elegant, "A City of Debris and Corpses," *Time*, January 10, 2005, http://www.time.com/time/.
4. Ibid.
5. The story was told at the Valparaiso Conference on Sports and Ethics, February 10, 2004, held in Chicago, Illinois.

Chapter 9: The Joy of Unfulfilled Desire

1. Gregory of Nyssa, *Life of Moses*, translation, introduction, and notes by Abraham J. Malherbe and Everett Ferguson (Mahwah, NJ: Paulist, 1978) bk. II, par. 233, p. 115.
2. A. W. Tozer, *Knowledge of the Holy: The Attributes of God: Their Meaning in the Christian Life* (New York: Harper & Brothers, 1961), 17.
3. Augustine, *Confessions*, book 2, 6:14, from *Confessions and Enchiridion*, http://www.fordham.edu/halsall/basis/confessions-bod.html.
4. Belden Lane, *The Solace of Fierce Landscapes: Exploring Desert and Mountain Spirituality* (New York: Oxford University Press, 1998), 210.
5. Ibid., 146.
6. Gregory of Nyssa, *Life of Moses*, bk. II, par. 233, p. 115.
7. Tozer, *Knowledge of the Holy*, 16.

Chapter 10: Sobering Power

1. Dillard, "Expedition to the Pole," in *Teaching a Stone to Talk*, 40.
2. James B. Smith, *Embracing the Love of God: The Path and Promise of the Christian Life* (San Francisco: HarperSanFrancisco, 1995), http://www.amazon.com/exec/obidos/ASIN/0060667419/qid=1123888254/sr=2-1/ref=pd_bbs_b_2_1/103-8649965-6099023.
3. The quotations in this and the following paragraph are taken from a sermon given by Frank Griswold, the presiding bishop of the Episcopal Church (ECUSA), at St. Paul's Cathedral, London, September 12, 2004. A transcript of the sermon can be found online: "Presiding Bishop Preaches in London," Episcopal News Service, http://www.episcopalchurch.org/3577_50505_ENG_HTM.htm.
4. Peterson, *Long Obedience in the Same Direction*, 116.
5. G. K. Chesterton, *The Everlasting Man* (1925; repr., New York: Dodd, Mead, & Company, 1953), 102.

Chapter 11: Mercifully Irrelevant

1. Søren Kierkegaard, "The Offense," in *Provocations: Spiritual Writings of Kierkegaard*, comp. and ed. Charles E. Moore (Farmington, PA: Plough Publishing House, 1999), 171–72.

2. Andy Crouch, "Thou Shalt Be Cool: This Enduring American Slang Leaves Plenty Out in the Cold," *Christianity Today*, March 11, 2002, 72.

3. Donald Miller, *Blue Like Jazz: Non-Religious Thoughts on Christian Spirituality* (Nashville: Thomas Nelson, 2003), 211.

4. Kierkegaard, "The Offense," 171–72.

5. Dietrich Bonhoeffer, *Life Together*, trans. John W. Doberstein (New York: Harper & Row, 1954), 27.

6. Ibid.

Chapter 12: *Really* High-Demand Religion

1. Dietrich Bonhoeffer, *The Cost of Discipleship* (1937; rev. and abridged, New York: MacMillan, 1959), 60.

2. Dean Kelly, *Why Conservative Churches Are Growing: A Study in Sociology of Religion* (New York: HarperCollins, 1972).

3. Laurence R. Iannaccone, "Why Strict Churches Are Strong," *American Journal of Sociology* 99, no. 5 (March 1994): 1180–1211.

4. Ibid.

5. See especially Roger Finke and Rodney Stark, *The Churching of America, 1776–1990: Winners and Losers in Our Religious Economy* (New Brunswick, NJ: Rutgers University Press, 1993), and Rodney Stark, *The Rise of Christianity: How the Obscure, Marginal, Jesus Movement Became the Dominant Religious Force* (San Francisco: HarperSanFrancisco, 1997).

6. "A Double Take on Early Christianity: An Interview with Rodney Stark," National Institute for the Renewal of the Priesthood, July 22, 2004, http://www.jknirp .com/stark.htm.

7. Matthew Bunson, general ed., *2004 Our Sunday Visitor's Catholic Almanac*, (Huntington, IN: Our Sunday Visitor, 2004), 459. Friars Minor (16,642), Capuchins (11,465), and Conventuals (4,553) are the three major male Franciscan orders.

8. Rob Moll, "The New Monasticism: A Fresh Crop of Christian Communities Is Blossoming in Blighted Urban Settings All across America," *Christianity Today*, September 2005, 38.

Chapter 13: Gracious Impatience

1. Dean Waldt, "The Myth of the Tolerant God," Presbyterians for Renewal, http://www.pfrenewal.org/publications_details_articles.asp?q_publicationid=45&q_articleid=36&q_areaid=6.

2. James R. Edwards, *The Gospel According to Mark* (Grand Rapids: Eerdmans, 2002), 235.

3. Quotations in this and the following paragraph are taken from Martin Luther King Jr., *Letter from a Birmingham Jail*, April 23, 1963, found at http://www.sas.upenn.edu/African_Studies/Articles_Gen/Letter_Birmingham.html, among many other websites.

Chapter 14: Harsh Tutors of Love

1. Don Terry, "I'm the One Who Makes the Noise," *Chicago Tribune Magazine*, January 30, 2005, 14–15.
2. Jack Nelson-Pallmeyer, *Is Religion Killing Us? Violence in the Bible and the Quran* (New York: Trinity Press International, 2003), 63.
3. Aquinas and Calvin, quoted in Darrel Cole, "Good Wars," in *First Things* 116 (October 2001): 27–31.
4. John Charles Selner, *The Teaching of St. Augustine on Fear as a Religious Motive* (Baltimore: St. Mary's University, 1937).
5. Augustine, *Epistle of John*, IX, n. 4, quoted in ibid., 62.

Chapter 15: The Storm before the Calm

1. Augustine, *Confessions*, book 8, 9:25, from *Confessions and Enchiridion*, http://fordham.edu/halsall/basis/confessions-bod.html.
2. Ibid., 7:16.
3. Ibid., 8:19, 20.
4. Ibid., 11:25.
5. Ibid., 12:28.
6. Ibid., 11:25.

Chapter 16: Forsaken by Grace

1. Teresa of Avila, *The Interior Castle*, 3.18, as quoted in Tessa Bielecki, *Teresa of Avila: Mystical Writings* (New York: Crossroad, 1994), 141.
2. Susan Shelley, "Unshakable Love: Our Family's Life-and-Death Struggles Tested Whether We Had This 'Unshakable Love,'" *Marriage Partnership*, Winter 1996, 52.
3. David Scott, "Finding Joy in the Darkest Night: The Divine Abandonment of Mother Teresa," on Godspy.com, July 29, 2005, http://www.godspy.com/reviews/Finding-Joy-in-the-Darkest-Night-The-Divine-Abandonment-of-Mother-Teresa-by-David-Scott.cfm.
4. Anthony Bloom, *Beginning to Pray* (Mahwah, NJ: Paulist, 1970), 29.
5. Ibid.

Chapter 17: Fearsome Love

1. Dillard, "God in the Doorway," in *Teaching a Stone to Talk*, 141.
2. St. Francis of Assisi, "Canticle of Brother Sun," from *Francis and Clare: The Complete Works*, trans. Regis J. Armstrong and Ignatius C. Brady (Mahwah, NJ: Paulist Press, 1982), 38.
3. Lane, *Solace of Fierce Landscapes*, 180.

DISCUSSION QUESTIONS FOR SMALL GROUPS

Each discussion can begin with these general questions:

What sentence, illustration, or idea was most compelling to you?

Where do you find yourself disagreeing with the author? Why?

And end the discussion with:

What is one thing you want to take away from this chapter?

Chapter 1: Difficult Love

1. Which do you identify with most: Jesus's experience at baptism or in the wilderness?

2. Describe a time when the love of God was an immediate experience for you.

3. Are such experiences a normal part of the Christian life, or are they extraordinary?

4. Describe a time of adversity that has troubled you.

5. Did you ever come to a point when you discerned God's hand in the adversity?

6. Some people object to the idea that God would lead us into adversity (like Jesus) or deliberately permit it to happen to us (like Job). What are the consequences for our theology if we take this view?

7. What are the types of adversities in which it is easiest to see God's hand? When is it hardest to see God's hand?

8. Do you think all suffering can end in loving service? Are there some forms of suffering that simply cannot be redeemed this side of God's kingdom?

9. Why do some suffering people more easily move toward redemptive action while others remain bitter and see only meaningless pain?

10. Regarding the firefighter analogy at the end of the chapter: In what ways is this fitting to the chapter's conclusion? In what ways does it not apply? Can you think of another analogy that makes the same point?

Chapter 2: A Hopeful Repentance

1. Do you picture the summary of Jesus's message in Mark 1:15 as stern and hard-hitting or gentle and inviting?

2. Do you think such phrases as "there is no health in us" and "miserable offenders" should be resurrected in our prayers of confession? Why or why not?

3. What do you consider to be "man-made religious taboos" that bother Christians but in the end are really not sins in your mind?

4. Are there examples of "false guilt" with which you have struggled or continue to wrestle?

5. How would it change the church's preaching, teaching, and worship if we were to emphasize the gospel as "the repentance that leads to life"? Would such a change be positive or negative?

6. Eugene Peterson says that repentance is "a renunciation of the lies we have been told about ourselves and our neighbors and our universe." What are the lies we are told about ourselves? About our neighbors? About our universe?

7. Ambrose said, "Shame indeed there is when each makes known his sins, but that shame, as it were, ploughs his land, removes the ever-recurring brambles, prunes the thorns, and gives life to the fruits which he believed were dead." Do we need to *feel* shame or remorse to be genuinely repentant? Or do we need to merely be sincere, regardless of feelings?

8. Frederica Mathewes-Green says, "We must stop thinking of God as infinitely indulgent. We must begin to grapple with the scary and exhilarating truth that he is infinitely holy, and that he wants the same for us." How do we combine this truth with the biblical theme, "The mercy of the Lord is from everlasting to everlasting"?

Chapter 3: Holy War

1. Does the author's characterization of Jesus as a soldier invading Satan's territory make sense to you? How does this alter your view of Jesus?

2. The warfare metaphor has been commonly used throughout church history ("Onward Christian Soldiers" and so forth), but it has fallen out of favor in the last half-century. Why? What has the church given up in abandoning this metaphor? What has it gained?

3. The word *holy* and the phrase "a life of holiness" are out of fashion today in many circles. Why is that?

4. Augustine wrote, "For out of the perverse came lust, and the service of lust ended in habit, and habit, not resisted, became necessity. Unruly habit kept saying to me, 'Do you think you can live without them?'" What concrete steps can we take to begin resisting such habits?

5. Have you ever had an experience of Jesus's holy love when you felt he was putting the pressure on to get you to deal with a sin, habit, or behavior?

6. Have you ever felt this pressure when it comes to a calling he wanted you to pursue?

7. "In the beginning, there are a great many battles and a good deal of suffering for those who are advancing towards God," wrote the desert mother known as Amma Syncletica, "and afterwards, ineffable joy." Have you had a similar experience in any area of your life?

Chapter 4: Prayer Scandals

1. Describe a particularly moving or meaningful prayer time that you have experienced.

2. Have you ever felt like one of the saints, such as Julian of Norwich, when you felt like bursting out, "I saw him and sought him! I had him and I wanted him"?

3. Can you think of other examples when you or an acquaintance "abandoned" family and loved ones for the sake of the gospel?

4. How can we determine when such a call is not merely an excuse to avoid one's godly responsibilities toward family and friends?

5. Was it fair or right for Morrison's mother to extract a promise from him not to go overseas until she had died? Are there any circumstances when limiting another's actions is justified?

6. What is the most unusual, perhaps even scandalous, thing that you have done as the result of prayer?

Chapter 5: It's Not Nice to Be Nice

1. If Catherine of Siena had asked you how she should act when she met the pope, how would you have advised her? What is the typical advice one would give to someone who is about to meet a famous and powerful person?

2. Why do you suppose Catherine got away with insulting Pope Gregory XI like this?

3. Why do you suppose Jesus speaks so firmly and harshly to people during his healings?

4. We live in a time when "civility" is a cardinal virtue. What are the positives and negatives in encouraging everyone to speak civilly with one another?

5. What is the difference between "love your neighbor as yourself" and "be nice to your neighbor as you would have him be nice to you"?

6. Can you think of an example where niceness actually made things worse?

7. Can you think of an example where getting angry only made things worse?

8. How might we determine when we have been nice enough long enough and when it is time to speak more boldly or harshly?

Chapter 6: Love That Makes Enemies

1. Paul tells us to "Live at peace with everyone" (Rom. 12:18 NIV), and Jesus says that peacemakers are blessed (Matt. 5:9). Yet both Paul and Jesus ended up creating a lot of conflict and hostility. How can we understand this paradox?

2. Do you believe that faithful Christians will usually be persecuted, no matter their cultural context? Or is persecution an extraordinary event?

3. Discuss examples of inappropriately stirring up trouble.

4. Discuss examples of when you or an acquaintance inappropriately refused to speak the truth or act boldly because of the desire to "keep the peace."

5. Can you think of an example when you have spoken truthfully, even kindly, to another and he or she didn't take it well?

6. Who are Christians today who are doing things in Jesus's name that offend others? What do these people have in common? What can we learn from them?

Chapter 7: Wretched Individualism

1. In what ways is Francis' story still a very modern story?

2. What types of Christian behavior tend to scandalize nominal believers and unbelievers today?

3. What are examples of spiritual enthusiasm gone awry today?

4. The Reformation was a key moment when many people began to recognize the value and responsibility of the individual before God. What is good about emphasizing the individual person of faith?

5. What are some examples where individualism has gotten out of hand in our culture? In the church?

6. If anyone didn't seem to "need" community, it was Jesus. Yet he always surrounded himself with disciples. Why?

7. What are ways to commit yourself to living out the faith less as a lone individual and more in the context of "brothers and sisters and mothers"?

Chapter 8: Good Warnings

1. If Jesus sternly warned people as much as the author argues, how does that alter your view of Jesus?

2. What is the most helpful warning you have ever received?

3. Why are we so hesitant to warn people about spiritual and moral dangers today?

4. When does lovingly warning others about their behavior drift into merely being a busybody?

5. What types of things do we have to do to earn the right to warn others?

6. What are warnings the church in general should be hearing today? What warnings should your local church be hearing?

7. What warnings do you think Jesus might be giving *you* today?

Chapter 9: The Joy of Unfulfilled Desire

1. What is the most intriguing, mysterious, yet fascinating aspect of Jesus to you?

2. A. W. Tozer wrote: "The yearning to know What cannot be known, to comprehend the Incomprehensible, to touch and taste the Unapproachable, arises from the image of God in the nature of man." What are some aspects of God's character or reality in general that you want to comprehend?

3. We often tell people, paraphrasing Augustine, that our hearts are restless until they find rest in God. Yet, as Belden Lane sums up one thread of spiritual wisdom, "It is love's unattainability that draws us inexorably to it. Nothing is so unattainable as God, nothing more out of reach. Yet nothing evokes our love more strongly." How do we understand both of these insights—that we can find rest and that we will be eternally restless?

4. One of the church's tasks is to make the faith accessible to unbelievers so that they might understand the gospel and turn and believe. Is it possible that simplifying the faith can be overdone? What are some examples? Why is this a problem?

5. Why do we feel compelled to explain everything? Why are we uncomfortable with mystery?

6. What might the church do to make sure that Christian faith has this intriguing, mysterious element of longing and desire?

Chapter 10: Sobering Power

1. Do you think most people are uncomfortable with the power of Jesus?

2. What is your greatest temptation when it comes to the power of Christ: to spiritualize it, rationalize it, manipulate it, or subvert it (fold it into other themes)?

3. The author says we are tempted to sentimentalize God. What does that mean? How is that different from merely feeling emotionally warm toward God, which most would assume is an appropriate experience?

4. Can you give an example of when you felt a type of fear that was in the end a positive experience? Is there a parallel with your relationship with God?

5. Many people believe the biblical passages about the fear of the Lord are really about holding God in awe. The author thinks there is a difference between the fear and awe of God. How would you describe the difference? Do you believe we need both?

6. What can people do to instill in themselves a deeper fear of the Lord and a greater sense of his power?

Chapter 11: Mercifully Irrelevant

1. Do you believe Jesus tried to be relevant to his culture? Why or why not?

2. Why are we in the church so anxious to be relevant to the culture?

3. What are the positives and negatives of targeting certain groups for outreach?

4. What might be signs that the desire to be relevant has gone too far?

5. What are the typical signs of success for a church? In what ways might they show genuine spiritual effectiveness? In what ways might they hide some serious spiritual flaws?

6. Søren Kierkegaard wrote, "Woe to the person who smoothly, flirtatiously, commandingly, convincingly preaches some soft, sweet something which is supposed to be Christianity! Woe to the person who makes miracles reasonable. Woe to the person who betrays and breaks the mystery of faith, distorts it into public wisdom, because he takes away the possibility of offense! . . . Oh the time wasted in this enormous work of making Christianity so reasonable, and in trying to make it so relevant!" Where do you see this happening today?

7. Can you think of an example, historically or from your own experience, of someone who was irrelevant by contemporary standards but was especially effective for Christ?

Chapter 12: *Really* High-Demand Religion

1. Jesus was both a high-demand teacher and a high-mercy Messiah. How do you reconcile these two seemingly contradictory realities?

2. What demands do you think your church should be requiring of its members? What should be required of *you?*

3. Are there any ways in which your church is too demanding? Can you give any examples of when you have seen a church overdo it?

4. Sometimes making high demands just feels demanding. Other times, we see it as an act of love. What is the difference?

5. Why is it so easy to see mercy as an act of love but so hard to see that expecting the most of others is also love?

6. How can your church start to make more Christlike demands on its members without becoming legalistic or self-righteous?

Chapter 13: Gracious Impatience

1. Do you agree with the author that Jesus showed impatience often? How does that alter your view of Jesus?

2. Some would say Jesus, as perfect God and man, has the right to be impatient, but fallible human beings do not have that right. Do you agree? Why or why not?

3. What people or circumstances make the most demands on your patience?

4. Do you think it would ever be appropriate to express impatience in these situations?

5. Can you think of an instance when patience did more harm than good?

6. What are signs that impatience is less about loving confrontation and more about irritability?

7. What are some issues or concerns about which you think the church should stop being patient?

Chapter 14: Harsh Tutors of Love

1. Do you believe, as the author argues, that Jesus sometimes motivated others by fear and shame? If so, does that change your perception of Jesus?

2. Can you think of an example when someone used fear or shame to motivate but it was completely inappropriate?

3. How about an instance when it worked to the good?

4. Under what circumstances do you think it is appropriate to motivate by fear or shame?

5. Does perfect love cast out fear this side of God's kingdom, or will we always have to be motivated by some level of fear in this life?

Chapter 15: The Storm before the Calm

1. What are some other New Testament instances when, as Jesus drew near, things became more unnerving, more uncomfortable for people?

2. Have you had this experience in your own life?

3. Do you think God is *in* the storms of life, or is it that he comes to us *after* the storms of life?

4. Jesus promises peace to those who draw near to him. Yet when Jesus is near, there can often be calamity. How do you understand this paradox?

5. Theologically, the injustice perpetrated on Jesus has no parallel, and yet we still *feel* that some injustices today are greater. Why is that?

6. Does it comfort you more to know that Jesus empathizes with your suffering or that he has power to redeem your suffering?

7. When people describe to us a storm in their own lives, should we tell them the biblical truth that Jesus might be near? Or should we simply listen empathetically because saying this at that time would sound like a cheap platitude?

Chapter 16: Forsaken by Grace

1. What are the various things you would hope that God would do for you if you hung on a cross like Jesus?

2. What are the various types of forsakenness Jesus probably experienced?

3. Has it been true for you that your early Christian walk was characterized by a more immediate sense of God's presence? And has this sense left you over the years? Or is the experience of losing the sense of God's presence only reserved for "saints"?

4. Do mature Christians experience the presence of God differently, and if so, how?

5. Is it important to have an emotional sense of God's presence, or is it more important to live by mere faith?

6. How do you experience God's absence? As a functional atheist—you've more or less gotten used to it? Or do you sometimes feel abandoned by God?

7. The author argues that coming to know Christ intimately means coming to know his forsakenness. Do you think this is true? If so, how does that make you feel about following Christ?

8. Is this common experience of forsakenness for Christians something we should let people know before they decide to follow Jesus? Why or why not?

Chapter 17: Fearsome Love

1. What notions about Jesus have had to die within you as you worked your way through this book?

2. What notions have been given new life?

3. What are aspects of Jesus's character that continue to puzzle, bother, or intrigue you?

4. When all is said and done, has the author made his case? Or is the bigger problem still the need to remind people of the gentleness and kindness of God?

5. If you agree with the author, what changes might have to be made in Christian education, preaching, and the church's mission to bring out this aspect of God's love?

Mark Galli is the managing editor of *Christianity Today*. He is the author or coauthor of several books, including *131 Christians Everyone Should Know* and *Francis of Assisi and His World*.